THROWN POTTERY
TECHNIQUES
Revealed

THROWN POTTERY
TECHNIQUES
Revealed

The secrets of perfect throwing shown in
unique cutaway photography

Mary
Chappelhow

**krause
publications**

700 E. State Street • Iola, WI 54990-0001

A QUARTO BOOK

Copyright (c) 2001 Quarto Inc.

ISBN 0-87349-346-X

**krause
publications**

700 East State Street, Iola, WI 54990-0001

Please call or write for our free catalog of publications. Our toll-free number to place an order or obtain a free catalog is 80-0-258-0929, or please use our regular business telephone, 715-445-2214.

QUAR.TPOT

This book was designed and produced by
Quarto Publishing plc
The Old Brewery
6 Blundell Street
London N7 9BH

Project editor Marie-Claire Muir
Art editor Julie Francis
Designer Julie Francis
Assistant art director Penny Cobb
Photographer Ian Howes
Illustrator Sherri Tay
Styling Plum Partnership Design Consultants
Copy editor Claire Waite
Proofreader Deirdre Clark
Indexer Diana Le Core
Art director Moira Clinch
Publisher Piers Spence

Manufactured by Universal Graphics, Singapore
Printed by Leefung-Asco Printers Trading Limited, China

Contents

Introduction

Learning to throw is generally thought to be a difficult and complex process, but with clear instruction, and a little practice, throwing techniques can easily be learned. Knowledge of even a few basic techniques will enable the reader to create a wide range of ceramic objects.

The book is divided into sections. To begin with, it informs the reader of the equipment needed to start throwing and advises on clays. Detailed instructions and step-by-step photographs show how to prepare clay for throwing, along with various wedging and kneading techniques.

The next section deals with centering, opening, and lifting the clay, and the reader is shown the main techniques, and some variations, used by different potters. There is more than one way to get the same result, so it is left to the individual to try the different methods in this section to decide what works best for them.

The main body of the book is devoted to throwing projects. These are featured in order of difficulty, starting with a simple straight vase and ending with a teapot. The projects have been designed to cover

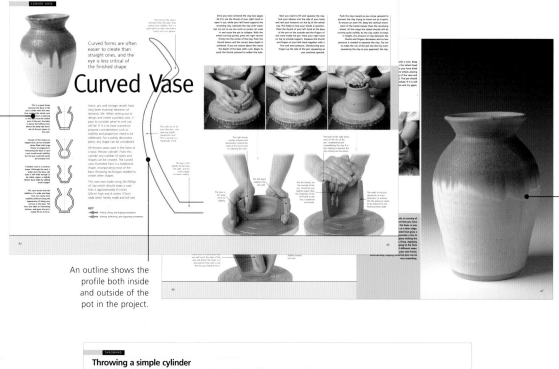

At the beginning of each project alternative forms from the same family are discussed. These provide alternative shapes for the potter to try later.

An outline shows the profile both inside and outside of the pot in the project.

Finished photographs show what you can achieve with a little practice.

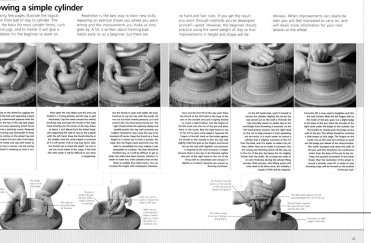

Step-by-step photographs show every part of the throwing process clearly and logically.

The cutaway photographs show what is happening on the inside of the pot, and reveal the hand positions that normally would be unseen during throwing.

Health and safety

Throwing is not generally a dangerous pastime, but a few basic, commonsense rules should be observed to keep you safe and sound.

a range of throwing techniques, giving the potter the knowledge needed to go on to create their own individual work. Each project is designed to encourage the potter to create a highly finished piece of work, and shows all the relevant information to achieve this. Throughout the projects, cutaway photographs are displayed in conjunction with step-by-step text and photography to show what is happening on the inside of the pot, as well as the hand positions on the outside. Each project also features a list of other suggested shapes in the same family. The projects can all be tackled individually, so experienced potters could go straight to the more complicated projects, rather than working through from the beginning of the book.

The subsequent sections illustrate various finishing processes, designed to provide a source of inspiration to the potter and encourage the creation of unique pieces. The main techniques for turning, creating surface patterns, and making lids, handles, and knobs are displayed and provide a wealth of ideas for the potter to pick and choose from.

- Never eat or drink in the workshop.
- Always tie back long hair to avoid it getting trapped in the rotating wheel.
- Secure loose clothing before using the wheel.
- Always use dry hands to switch electrical equipment on and off.
- Wear gloves when using any coloring agents or oxides.
- Wear a respirator (face mask) when using any powders.

Wet clay is not particularly dangerous, but dry clay—which can form dust when crushed under foot or collect on surfaces—can be. Clay dust can be very fine and contains silica which, if breathed in, can cause, over time, silicosis of the lungs. The best way to avoid breathing in clay dust is to avoid making it in the first place by following these basic principles:

- Wash down clay preparation surfaces while they are still damp, straight after use.
- If clay or turnings end up on the floor, clean them up immediately.
- Never sweep a floor, always vacuum a dry floor with an absolute filter fitted to collect fine dust, or, even better, clean with a wet mop.
- Wear protective clothing, but try not to wipe dirty hands on aprons because when the wipings dry they will flake off and cause dust. Always wash clothing after every session at the wheel.
- If you sand down dry or biscuit-fired pots, be sure to wear a respirator (face mask) with a suitable filter for clay dust (silica dust).

Beware

Certain colorants and materials can be added to clay before it is thrown to change its properties or color. Extra care should be taken when using the following materials:

Highly toxic
Lead
Cadmium
Antimony
Barium

Use with care
Borax, boron, boric acid
Silica, quartz, flint, feldspar, china clay, ball clay
Whiting, dolomite
Cobalt oxide and carbonate
Copper oxide and carbonate
Chromium oxide
Lithium oxide
Zinc
Strontium
Nickel oxide
All other colorants and metal oxides

All materials should be used with some degree of caution. Pottery suppliers can provide the relevant health and safety data for all their products. Each material will have information relating to the contents printed on the bag it is supplied in, so do read them.

Tools

Many pottery tools can be made at home, but on the whole they are usually purchased from pottery suppliers. Below are the most commonly used tools for throwing.

As you work through the techniques in this book, you will discover which are the best tools for you and the job in hand. Every potter has their own toolkit, containing a mix of handmade, modified, or shop-bought tools.

It is not necessary to spend lots of money on tools, as a few basics will suffice to start throwing. Making your own tools can be very cheap and also rewarding because you can make the exact shape that you require. One throwing rib, one sponge, a wire, and a ribbon tool are all you need to tackle most basic throwing projects.

Bamboo tools
These are used for sealing joins in pots and for creating different surface textures. They can also be used to model clay.

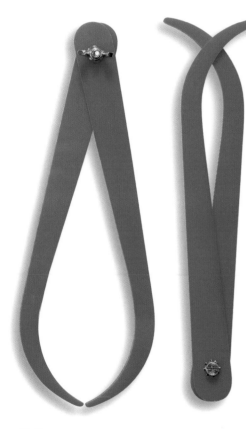

Calipers
These are most often used for measuring the width of lids and galleries. The calipers can be set to a particular width and put aside until needed later.

Craft knife
A craft knife is always useful to have to hand and can be used to trim clay or to cut decoration.

Hole cutter
These are used to cut circular holes in leather-hard, part dry, clay, such as strainer holes in teapots.

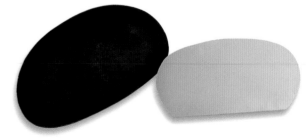

Kidneys
Kidneys can be used to either smooth the surface of wet pots or to remove clay during turning when the pot is leather hard (firm to the touch, but still damp). They are always made from metal, but come in different shapes and grades (thicknesses).

Sponge on a stick

A practical tool used to remove water from inside tall or narrow forms to avoid distorting the form with the hands.

Pin on a stick

This is a useful tool for trimming the rims of uneven pots, cutting through leather-hard, part dry, pots, pricking air bubbles that sometimes occur, and measuring the depth of the base of a pot.

Sponges

Whether natural or manmade, sponges are used to remove water from pots, smooth rims, and clean surfaces. A selection of sponges is essential to any potter.

Paint scraper

A household paint scraper is a useful tool for cleaning benches and boards. It can also be used to remove wooden bats from the wheel, clean the wheel head quickly, shape wet clay, and to create a bevel under a wet pot on the wheel.

Wire

A wire is used to cut through clay, whether this is during wedging or when removing pots from the wheel. The wire can be metal or plastic, but should have wooden toggles on either end to grip.

Ribbon tools

These tools are so called because they remove ribbons of clay from leather-hard pots during turning. They are metal loops on a wooden handle and come in many different shapes.

Triangular ribbon tool

This turning tool is used to trim away clay from leather-hard, part dry, pots and to create a bevel at the base of a wet or leather-hard pot.

Throwing ribs

Throwing ribs can be made from wood, metal, or plastic. You can make your own from old phone cards or buy wooden ones from suppliers. They are used for smoothing and shaping pots on the wheel.

Wheels

The potter's wheel has been in use for about 4,000 years: first in Egypt and then throughout the Middle East.

Wheels were originally made from a wooden disc placed on a wooden bearing and were turned by hand. Potters' wheels today are very much the same, except that they are now made from metal and most are powered by electricity. Some potters still prefer to use a foot-powered wheel, or momentum wheel, as they are sometimes called. These are usually cheaper to buy and obviously cheaper to run, but can be difficult to control when first learning to throw; concentrating on hand and foot movements at the same time is quite complicated. It is therefore recommended that the beginner starts on an electric wheel that will allow them to fully concentrate on the hand movements and gaining control over the clay.

When choosing a wheel, the main consideration should be your own comfort. Although you will have to bend your back to a certain extent, try to find a wheel that lets you hold your back as straight as possible; most do have adjustable seat heights. Pottery suppliers usually have a range of wheels to choose from at various prices. If possible, try them before you buy so you know which is right for you.

Unless you intend to make very large pots, the wheel does not have to be very powerful or large. You should also consider where you are going to keep the wheel before you buy one that is too large. Do you have the space to keep it in the workshop all the time, or does it need to be stored away when not in use?

It is possible to pick up a good secondhand wheel, advertisements for which can be found in pottery and craft magazines. If possible, take someone that knows about wheels or electrics to see the wheel and check it over before you buy—though most potters are, of course, perfectly trustworthy!

Types of wheel

Leach wheel
This is also a treadle wheel, but it has a seat to sit on. It is usually referred to as a Leach wheel, after Bernard Leach the famous potter who built it. It is operated by the foot bar, which is pushed back and forth.

Electric wheel
All the moving parts of this electric wheel are enclosed in the cabinet, a useful consideration if you have children. It also has safety buttons on the side to turn the power on and off. Pushing the accelerator bar down operates the wheel. The further down the accelerator the faster the wheel turns. This wheel is very large, but a good design for all sizes of pottery production.

Small electric wheel
This is a smaller version of the electric wheel, and is often sold to beginners or hobby potters. It is small, light, easily stored, and the seat is removable. It is simple to operate, by pressing down on the accelerator pedal. It has a large water tray to collect stray clay and water.

Treadle wheel
This is an inexpensive wheel that is operated in a sitting position. The bar is pushed in and out with the foot. This can be awkward, since, in effect, you have to power the wheel, and throw the clay all at once.

Shimpo
This Japanese-style wheel is quite powerful, but small and easy to store. Very tall pots can be made on them because the potter is able to stand up and continue to raise the pot as it becomes taller. The foot pedal operates the wheel. The further you press it down the faster it goes.

Note
- Make sure the wheel tray does not overfill with water during throwing, as this could cause the bearing of the wheel head to become wet and cause it to rust.
- Wheels should never be turned off and on at the socket with wet hands.

Shimpo

Electric wheel

Treadle wheel

Clays

The chemistry of clay is a complex subject. Here is just a brief outline of the most important facts you need to know when selecting clay for throwing.

Clay in its natural state can be found almost everywhere. It is most visible on riverbanks where water has eroded the bank, and can be found in most gardens if you dig deep enough. The two essential elements of clay are silica and alumina, which originate from igneous rock. Most clays begin as feldspathic or granite rock, which has decomposed and weathered over millions of years. Some remain where they were originally formed and are known as "primary" clays. Others are carried by water and deposited far away from their point of origin in sedimentary layers, and are known as secondary clays.

Primary clays are very pure, but rare. They are, on the whole, unsuitable for throwing in their natural state because their particle size is large, which tends to make them non-plastic. When added to other clays, however, they become workable and are, because of their whiteness, the main ingredient of other clay bodies, such as porcelain.

Secondary clays have very fine particles, and so are plastic. In travels from their place of origin they pick up various other minerals and impurities, which give them different qualities depending on where they have traveled and where they are deposited. Red clays, for example, contain the most common of minerals, iron oxide, which occurs the world over.

Throwing clay

Different clays are used for different pottery techniques. Here we will only discuss those suitable for throwing. Clay can be dug up straight from the ground and used for throwing, though it is rare to find a clay that is suitable—they are either non-plastic or too plastic. To test clay, roll a little in the hand and then bend it into a curve. If it breaks, or lots of splitting occurs, it is probably non-plastic and will need a more plastic clay, such as ball clay, added to it (up to 30 percent) to make it workable. If it is too sticky it could be combined with up to 10 percent of a non-plastic clay, such as grog (ground and fired clay), or sand to give it more workability on the wheel.

Digging your own clay can be rewarding, but until you know the requirements of clay for throwing it may be self-defeating. Digging clay is also labor intensive, as is the processing, which is the same as reclaiming (see page 14), and altering clay bodies so they are usable is time consuming. Many potters do prefer to mix their own personal clay bodies and will tell you they are better than anything commercially available. This may be true, but a lot of knowledge must be acquired before you can make your own clay, and to produce large amounts requires some fairly expensive equipment. So, to start with, it is a good idea to buy your clay ready-made. In time, you may feel the need to go that stage further. When you do, you can refer to one of the many good books on the subject of clay bodies, since it is too involved a subject to explore in detail here.

Ready-made clays

There are more and more pottery suppliers springing up that supply everything a potter requires, including clays. If you live near a supplier, it is best to collect the clay yourself since it is heavy and therefore costly to have delivered. If not, ask the supplier for a sample before you order a large amount. Clay suppliers usually have catalogs with descriptions of the clays they produce and examples of the fired colors. If, however, your nearest supplier does not, phone them to discuss your requirements and ask for a clay that is suitable for a beginner and is easy to throw. Usually they will be able to advise you on the firing temperatures and maturing temperatures of the clay as well. The clay will be supplied in a sealed plastic bag, ready to use.

Clay types

The array of clays can be confusing, and you need to consider what you want to make and the final result you hope to achieve before you choose one. Do you want a smooth white surface on which to decorate, or a rough, tactile, unglazed finish? If you want to produce pots for the oven, for example, you will need to use clay that is resistant to thermal shock (ask your supplier for their recommendations). Clays for throwing are available in three main categories.

Earthenware

Red earthenware is the most common naturally occurring clay and therefore the least expensive. It has a maturing temperature range of around 1,832–2,156°F (1,000–1,180°C) and is porous when fired, which makes it excellent for garden pots or chimney pots. For use in the kitchen, however, pots need to be glazed to make them waterproof and hygienic. Red earthenware is usually easy to throw, and because it is inexpensive it is ideal for the beginner.

White earthenware clay is also commercially available. It doesn't occur naturally and is a little more expensive than red earthenware. It is ideal as a surface for decoration, but can be a little trickier to throw, as it is quite dense and less open in texture. White earthenware has a maturing range of about 1,940–2,156°F (1,060–1,180°C) and also remains porous without a glaze coating.

Stoneware

This clay, when fired, is dense and hard, like stones—hence the name. It has a maturing range of 2,192–2,372°F (1,200–1,300°C). Glaze makes the surface of this clay smoother, but is not always necessary because the clay is non-porous when fired to maturity. Stoneware clay is available in a variety of colors, from white to dark brown. Most are bodies prepared from plastic clays and ceramic minerals; some are smooth and others much coarser. Suppliers often have their own stoneware bodies especially prepared for throwing, which are supplied at the right moisture contents as well. These are ideal for the beginner, even though they are a little more expensive than red earthenware. This type of clay is often used in schools and colleges and is usually buff in color.

Porcelain

Porcelain for throwing is a man-made clay: plastic, white, high-firing clay is almost impossible to find naturally. Porcelain has a firing range of 2,264–2,462 °F (1,240–1,350°C). It can be opaque or translucent, if potted thinly. Porcelain can be glazed or left unglazed as it is impervious to water and has a very hard, dense finish. Throwing porcelain is quite a challenge and it is not recommended for the beginner. Even porcelain that has been prepared especially for throwing is not tolerant to the overuse of water during throwing and is not always strong enough to hold its shape on the wheel. It is also prone to distortion during firing. If you want a white surface it is best to use a white stoneware or earthenware rather than porcelain. Porcelain should be potted thinly to show off its delicate properties; turning away clay after throwing is the usual technique for achieving this.

Coloring clay

Clay can be colored using either naturally occurring oxides or commercially available stains. If you use a white body you will get the best results. Adding colors, however, tends to make the clay short (not as plastic) and difficult to use; this can be improved by storing the clay for a few months. Colors also tend to lower the firing temperature, so test a new color before making anything with it. Colors tend to be expensive so, as a rule, colored clays are only used for small items. Color can be kneaded in or mixed with a dry clay body before it is prepared. Care should be taken, as some colorants can be poisonous or easily absorbed through the skin (see Health and safety, page 7).

Clay consistency and storage

Clay for throwing should be soft enough to mold in the fingers without sticking to them. The correct consistency varies depending on how large a pot you are trying to make, and every potter has their preferred consistency of clay for throwing. It will soon become apparent what is right for you. Try the clay straight from the bag after kneading it (see pages 16–17), then alter it accordingly. Wedge in softer clay (see page 15) if it is too dry, or knead it on a plaster bat to remove some of the water if it is too soft. If the clay is very hard you may have to dry it out and use the reclaiming method (see page 14) to make it pliable.

Clay should be stored in tightly sealed plastic bags to keep it damp, and in a dark, cool, but frost-free place. Even clay in plastic bags will dry out eventually, though it will remain usable if softened or reclaimed.

First mix the chosen colorant powder with water to make a thick paste. A mask is worn to prevent breathing in any powder and gloves are worn to protect the hands.

A block of porcelain is cut into slices. The paste is then spread onto the layers.

The layers are then put together and kneaded until the color is evenly distributed throughout the clay body. This colored clay would be best left for a couple of weeks before using, as it can be very short and unsuitable for throwing immediately. Store the newly mixed clay in an air tight bag until required.

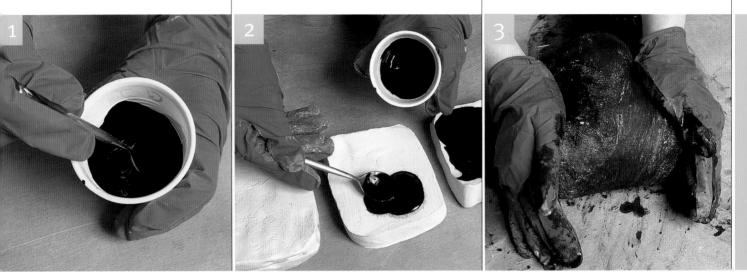

Raw clay

A very dark gray stoneware clay with flecks of iron dispersed throughout.

The high iron content gives red stoneware clay its color.

Porcelain is a very white clay.

A standard, buff-colored stoneware clay.

White earthenware is gray before it is fired.

Red earthenware.

Fired clay

The iron spots produce flecks of brown in the clay when it is fired.

The red stoneware becomes very dark red when fired.

When fired, porcelain is white and smooth.

The buff stoneware clay is a creamy color when fired.

The white earthenware turns white after firing.

Fired red earthenware is a rich terra-cotta color.

Shrinkage
Each of the clay tiles on the right had a 4-inch (10cm) line drawn in the raw clay before firing. This is used to measure shrinkage after firing. Most clays shrink by 10 percent from their raw state to mature fired. What seems like quite a large pot when it is first formed on the wheel can look considerably smaller when fired.

Reclaiming clay

The beauty of clay is that until it is fired it can be reused over and over again. There is no waste when learning to throw, as unsuccessful pots can be reclaimed and the clay reused. Turnings and wheel-tray slops can be reclaimed in the same way.

Processing dug clay

A technique very similar to reclaiming clay can also be used to process clay you have dug up yourself. Use more water to slake the clay down and form a thinner slurry rather than a slop. Pass the slurry through a sieve to remove stones and organic materials. Let the contents settle in the plastic container and pour or sponge off the excess water before placing the clay on a plaster bat. This clay, once it has been dried out to the right consistency, can then be wedged and kneaded until it is ready to use.

Leave clay to be reclaimed to dry out completely. This may take three or four days, depending on the size of the pieces. Break the dry clay into small pieces and place them in a large plastic container.

The clay then needs to be slaked down. To do this, cover the clay in the container with warm water and leave it to soften, preferably overnight.

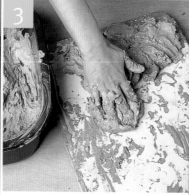

Pour or sponge off any excess water still on the surface. Mix the slop with your hand and cover a plaster bat with an even layer of slop, about 2 inches (5cm) deep. The plaster will absorb the water from the slop and therefore help the clay to dry out and firm up. The rate at which the plaster absorbs the water depends on how dry the bat was before the slop was added. Do this in the morning and keep an eye on how well the clay is firming up through-out the day.

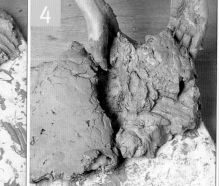

When the clay has started to firm up and can be easily pulled away from the bat, turn it over so the top surface then comes into contact with the plaster, to even up the drying process. As soon as the clay is of a workable consistency, remove it from the plaster bat and wedge and knead it (see pages 15–17), until it is ready to be reused. If the clay can be rolled and bent between the fingers without breaking, it is plastic enough to use. If it appears to crack it is "short" and will benefit from storage to regain its plasticity.

Contaminated clay

Be careful not to chip any plaster from the plaster bat, or contaminate the clay with small pieces of plaster. Plaster absorbs water; if any is mixed into the clay it can cause areas of clay to split away from the wall of the pot during firing.

Wedging clay

To combine two different clays, or a soft and hard clay, it is best to wedge it prior to kneading it. In this series of photographs, two contrasting clays have been used only to show how the wedging mixes the clays evenly together. This technique is usually used to combine uneven clay of the same sort to make it the right consistency for throwing.

Wedging is ideal for large pieces of clay. The process is not worth the effort for clay weighing less than approximately 10 lbs (4.5kg) because kneading on its own would probably be sufficient (see pages 16–17).

Wedging is best done on a very sturdy table, as it will have to withstand a lot of force placed on it. Ideally the table should be below your waist height so the clay has further to fall, allowing you to use less force.

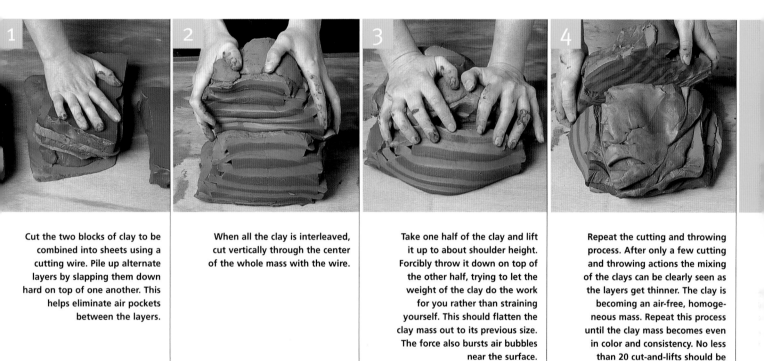

Cut the two blocks of clay to be combined into sheets using a cutting wire. Pile up alternate layers by slapping them down hard on top of one another. This helps eliminate air pockets between the layers.	When all the clay is interleaved, cut vertically through the center of the whole mass with the wire.	Take one half of the clay and lift it up to about shoulder height. Forcibly throw it down on top of the other half, trying to let the weight of the clay do the work for you rather than straining yourself. This should flatten the clay mass out to its previous size. The force also bursts air bubbles near the surface.	Repeat the cutting and throwing process. After only a few cutting and throwing actions the mixing of the clays can be clearly seen as the layers get thinner. The clay is becoming an air-free, homogeneous mass. Repeat this process until the clay mass becomes even in color and consistency. No less than 20 cut-and-lifts should be performed. The clay is now ready to knead (see pages 16–17).

Different techniques

Other pottery books will describe different ways of wedging clay. This technique is the most simple. Some potters cut the clay at an angle to create a wedge that is then thrown down, hence the name wedging, while others insist the clay should be constantly rotated as wedging continues. You will soon find the method that is easiest and gives you the best results.

Kneading

Wherever you get your clay supply from, it will need to be thoroughly prepared before use. Kneading clay well before you throw it is very important. Badly prepared or uneven clay can make throwing very difficult, or almost impossible, and is one of the main reasons for unsuccessful first attempts at the wheel.

Clay that arrives in plastic bags may seem even and ready to use, but the plastic draws water to the edges of the block of clay, leaving it dryer in the middle and wetter around the edges. Kneading will create a smooth, even lump of clay, and also remove air bubbles, which make throwing more difficult. However, kneaded clay

Ox-head kneading

The name of this kneading technique relates to the shape of the clay mass during kneading. This is the slightly easier of the two methods, though it is not suitable for large pieces of clay. Describing how to knead clay is difficult, as anyone who has tried to read a description of how to knead bread will know, so try to find someone to show you how to do it. In this series of photographs two contrasting clays have been used for the purpose of showing how the kneading successfully mixes the clay.

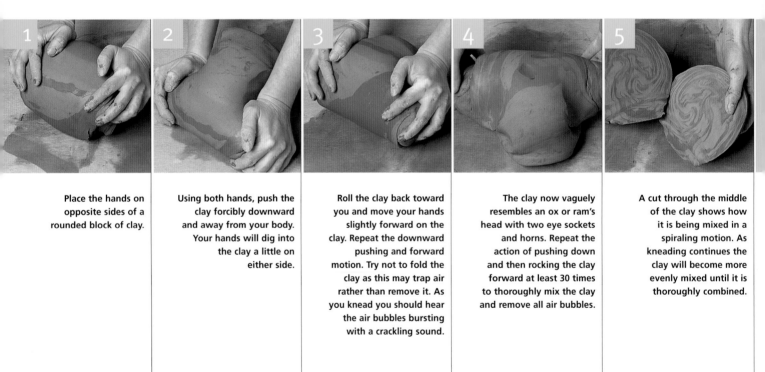

1	2	3	4	5
Place the hands on opposite sides of a rounded block of clay.	Using both hands, push the clay forcibly downward and away from your body. Your hands will dig into the clay a little on either side.	Roll the clay back toward you and move your hands slightly forward on the clay. Repeat the downward pushing and forward motion. Try not to fold the clay as this may trap air rather than remove it. As you knead you should hear the air bubbles bursting with a crackling sound.	The clay now vaguely resembles an ox or ram's head with two eye sockets and horns. Repeat the action of pushing down and then rocking the clay forward at least 30 times to thoroughly mix the clay and remove all air bubbles.	A cut through the middle of the clay shows how it is being mixed in a spiraling motion. As kneading continues the clay will become more evenly mixed until it is thoroughly combined.

does not stay evenly mixed for long, so only prepare the amount of clay you intend to use in the next hour or so. There are two methods of kneading, and it is up to you to decide which one you prefer.

Spiral kneading

During this technique the clay forms a spiral as the kneading continues. This method is more difficult to master but useful for larger pieces of clay and is an efficient method of mixing clay. In this series of photographs, two contrasting clays have been used only to show how the kneading successfully mixes the clay.

After kneading

Kneaded clay should be used for throwing immediately, since it will not stay even for long. Exposure to air starts to dry the surface of the clay as soon as kneading is completed. Even standing the clay on a wooden bench can start to dry it underneath, creating unevenness.

Form the clay into the size of balls you require and place those you don't want to use now in a sealed plastic bag. This keeps them at perfect consistency in the short term. Leaving them in a bag for any length of time (even overnight) will cause the clay to sweat and create unevenness, resulting in clay that is difficult to use on the wheel.

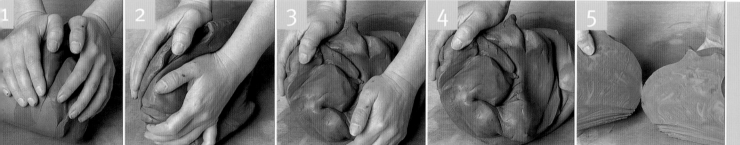

1 Place the hands on opposite sides of a rounded block of clay. Use the right hand to push down on the clay as it rolls forward, while the left hand stops the sideways movement of the clay and rotates it after each forward movement to create the spiral.

2 Push down on the clay with the right hand from above. The wrist of the right hand is put under a lot of pressure as it forces the clay downward. Try to use your upper body weight to aid this movement rather than using the wrist alone.

3 Use the left hand to rotate the clay by lifting and pivoting it counterclockwise while you move the right hand into position for the next downward push. Rock the body forward as you push down, and backward as the clay is lifted and turned to create a rhythm. You will use your body weight more efficiently if the table is below waist height. Compress the clay against the table to squeeze out the air. Do not fold the clay as you continue to knead, as you may trap more air rather than remove it.

4 A spiral can clearly be seen forming in the clay mass and the two types of clay are becoming less distinct. It is difficult to quantify how many rotations of the clay are needed to provide thorough mixing, but somewhere between 30 and 40 should do. Cut through the clay with a wire to check if any air bubbles are present and if there are still variations in the clay color. If there are, the two bodies are insufficiently mixed. Variations in consistency are more difficult to detect and it is only through practice that you will obtain this skill.

5 The complex mixing process can be clearly seen in this cross-section of the block of clay.

Throwing

Simply put, throwing is the shaping of a ball of clay by the hands, on a revolving wheel. This process, in the hands of an experienced potter, can look completely effortless; the pot appears out of the mass of revolving clay as if by magic. In reality, a few basic techniques have to be mastered before this ease can be achieved. These techniques, however, are not cast in stone. Ask a dozen potters how to perform a specific task and you will get 12 varying answers.

The following chapter covers the basics you need to go on to tackle the projects, but only through trying them out will you find the best method for you. Remember the clay can always be reclaimed (see page 14) if you are not happy with your results. Throwing can very quickly, with some determination, become second nature, so do not give up after the first attempt.

Centering

Centering involves pushing the ball of clay into the center of the wheel and smoothing its surface to ready it for throwing. There are various methods for centering clay, and learning to do so quickly and efficiently takes some practice.

Troubleshooting

• When a ball of clay is properly centered, it no longer has any movement. When the clay is spinning on the wheel, any wobble will be easy to spot once the hands are removed. If the hands move a great deal during centering, stop the wheel and examine the clay to check if it is properly centered. Try to push it back toward the center of the wheel before continuing.

• If the hands are moving around a lot, then they are not being held in place correctly. Make sure the forearms are resting on the wheel tray. Arms that are floating in space will be impossible to hold still as the clay rotates. If the hands are ridged, the clay is forced into the center.

Knead the clay (see pages 16–17), making it as even in consistency as possible and free from air. Weigh up some balls of clay. About 1 lb (500g) is an ideal place to start. Shape the clay into a cylinder or ball—the more round the clay is to start with, the easier it will be to center. Dampen the wheel head with water, but not too much, as this will stop the ball from sticking well and it may fly off. Throw the clay down directly in the center of the wheel, and ensure the it is well stuck down.

If your aim was not good, gently push the clay into the center. If it comes away from the wheel, then a little more force is required when throwing down. Keep water and a sponge nearby to dribble water onto the clay and hands whenever necessary.

method 1
Sit close to the wheel tray and tuck your elbows into the side of your body. Push the forearms gently onto the edge of the tray to lock them in position. Position your upper body over the clay so it is easier to exert downward pressure. If the wheel is revolving too slowly, the clay will control the hands rather than vice versa. There are a number of ways to center clay. Here, I use the side of the right hand to exert downward pressure on the top of the clay through its center, forcing it downward and outward. Hold the left hand steady in a vertical position against the wall of the clay mass, so as it widens it is smoothed, forcing any wobbles to be incorporated into the rotating clay. Using this method can force the clay to become too flat for opening.

method 2
As an alternative, cup the hands around the clay and squeeze it inward. Make sure the clay is well lubricated; if it is allowed to dry out it will snag on the hands and the clay will twist or tear from the wheel. The forearms should be resting on the wheel tray. Touching the thumbs together round the clay can help with stability. Squeeze the hands together to center the clay, exerting pressure from the wrists. If you squeeze too hard or the hands have become too dry, the clay may come off the wheel. If this happens, dry the hands and the wheel head a little, then form the clay into a ball and start again. This cetering method squeezes the clay inward so it will increase in height.

method 3
You can also combine downward and inward pressure techniques into one action. Cup the clay with the hands and squeeze inward, but use the thumbs on top of the clay to exert downward pressure. Let the thumbs touch and act as one. As they press down they will also create extra steadiness. This combined technique compresses the clay and speeds up the centering process. The clay should be pulled toward the body slightly to pull it into the center completely.

method 4
Alternatively, the clay can be pushed away from the body. Cup the clay with both hands and join the heels together to make them stronger. Force the clay forward into the center of the wheel and use the thumbs on top to stop the clay rising vertically. When your hands are on the clay you will be able to feel any bumps or wobbles with your fingers as the clay rotates. Continue to exert pressure on the clay until they are all eliminated. Once centered, remove the hands slowly from the spinning clay. Any sudden releases of pressure can cause the clay to wobble again. The clay needs to be completely central before throwing can proceed.

Coning up

This process is used to eliminate any unevenness that may be in the clay. It is not always necessary to do this, but it is a good technique to learn. It should never be a replacement for preparing clay correctly, but can help even out clay that has been kept under plastic for a few hours. This process also helps to align the clay particles into a spiral and may help make the clay easier to throw.

1 Center the clay. Place the hands around the clay at its base and squeeze them together. The clay is forced upward into a taller cone shape. The thumbs should only act as a support to the rising form. Be careful not to start with the clay too wide because when you push inward only the outside of the clay will be forced upward, leaving a hollow in the middle where water could gather and become incorporated in the clay. Lubricate the clay with water when needed.

2 Move the hands up the cone and continue to squeeze the clay inward and upward. Try to keep the arms on the edge of the wheel tray for support, as narrower forms are more likely to wobble. Overlap the fingers as the cone gets narrower to help hold the hands steady.

3 Place the right hand on top of the cone and exert a downward pressure, predominantly from the side of the hand. You can also use this movement to push the cone slightly away from the body, helping to keep the clay central. Hold the left hand firmly against the wall of the cone, thus preventing it from forming into a mushroom shape as it is forced downward. If a mushroom is formed the clay folds around itself, and the folds can trap water and air, creating problems later. Let the fingers of the right hand touch those of the left to give the clay no room to displace outward at the top of the cone, but cause the whole cone to become shorter and wider.

4 The cone has now been pushed back down by the side of the right hand supported by the left hand, and has returned to its initial shape. The process of lifting and dropping a cone should be repeated two or three times until the clay feels smooth and even.

5 Make sure the clay is central before forming continues. Press down on top of the the clay with the side of the right hand and push the left fingers under the base of the clay wall slightly to form a rough mushroom shape. It will now be easier to make a pot because there is less weight left at the base of the clay. If the clay is too wide at the base before throwing it is difficult to move up the pot later.

Opening

Each of the different opening methods results in the clay mass becoming a wall or "donut" of clay that can later be thinned. The most important part of this procedure is forming the base of the pot. The base should be ¼ inch (6mm) thick. If it is too thin, the wire used to cut the pot from the wheel may cut through the base. If the base is too thick, you will end up with a heavy pot or one that requires a lot of turning away later. Gauging the depth of the base comes with practice. If you are unsure, simply stick a pin through the base to measure it. The pinhole will seal up as throwing continues.

method 1
The wheel should be revolving fairly swiftly. Keep the clay lubricated. Support the clay with both hands and keep the forearms resting on the edge of the wheel tray. Push the thumb slowly into the center of the clay. Make sure it is directly in the middle of the clay, or a raised area may be left in the center of the base.

Push the thumb down until it is about ¼ inch (6mm) from the wheel head. This should give a reasonable depth of base. If you go too deep and can see or feel the wheel head, start again with a new ball of clay. Try not to use too much water on the inside at this stage. If the pot fills with water, it will be difficult to gauge the depth of the base.

Use the thumb to carefully force the clay outward and widen the hole, still supporting the clay wall on the outside with the left hand. Do this slowly, as any sudden or jerky movements may cause the pot to move off-center.

It takes a certain amount of pressure from the thumb to push the clay outward, but do not be tempted to rush this stage or lift the arms away from the wheel tray in an attempt to use more pressure. Try to keep the thumb at a constant height so that the depth of the base remains constant and flat.

method 2
If you find that one thumb is not strong enough, you can use two. Place the hands around the clay to support it, and hold the thumbs together to make them stronger. Push the thumbs into the center of the revolving clay. Keep them together until the correct depth of base has been reached; a hill of clay will be left in the middle of the base if they drift apart. You can also use both thumbs to widen the clay, though it can prove more difficult to control both hands at once, and it does tend to obscure the view of the bottom of the pot.

method 3
Rest the arms on the wheel tray, the right hand on the top of the clay, and the left hand on top of the right hand. Hold the fingers of the right hand firmly together and use the three middle fingers to open the clay. Place the middle finger directly in the center, then press downward with all three fingers. If you let them drift apart, a hill will form in the middle of the base. Once the fingers reach the correct depth, draw them toward you to open the clay further. Keep the thumb on the outside of the base behind the fingers as they pull the wall toward you, molding a wall as the clay is pushed outward to stop the clay from becoming too flat.

method 4
A different opening technique is required for low, wide forms. Center the clay lower and wider, and use the side of the right hand to displace the clay outward, pushing downward rather than making an opening. When the correct depth has been reached, push the hand outward to form a flat base and form a low, flat wall. When the hole is the required size, or the plate the required thickness, consolidate the base by running the fingers slowly back and forth across the base. Keep them flat and try not to cause ridges or displace the clay outward. Pressing down will compact the clay, making it stronger. This action helps prevent the formation of "S"-shaped cracks in the base during drying or firing.

Lifting the wall

The next stage of making a pot is to lift and stretch the wall of the pot to thin it and give the pot its height. There are again many methods of doing this. Here we will show the most popular. Throwing is about personal choice; no one way is the right way, try each method and choose what works for you.

Each method starts with clay that has already been opened and consolidated (see page 22).

method 1
Place the left-hand fingers on the inside, touching the wall at its base, and the left-hand thumb at the base on the outside. Gently squeeze together the thumb and fingers as the left hand slowly rises up the wall. It will only be possible to use this lift a couple of times, as the wall will become too high. A knuckle lift would be used next to lift the clay further.

method 2
Place the right thumb on the inside of the pot and the right fingers on the outside and squeeze them together as they travel up the wall to thin it. The left hand supports the wall on the opposite side. This lift is also limited by the height of the walls. It can be difficult to control the clay well, as the hands are not linked for extra support.

method 3
This is a variation on the previous method. The right thumb is placed inside the pot and the fingers on the outside. The thumb pushes out toward the fingers, which are lying horizontal on the outside of the pot in a crook shape. They too are pushed together to thin the clay, and the hooked finger pulls the bulge created by the thumb upward. This is used for a couple of preliminary lifts before the knuckle is used.

method 4
The fingers of the left hand are placed on the inside of the pot and the fingers of the right on the outside. The fingertips of the right hand squeeze the wall of the pot onto the fingers of the left hand inside the pot. The two sets of hands then rise up the wall together, squeezing the clay as they go. Repeat this lift to raise and thin the walls to their finished height. It can be a slow process, as a lot of clay cannot be moved upward at once. Be careful not to squeeze too hard, as the wall of the pot may snag on the fingers and tear.

method 5
This is the knuckle lift, used to efficiently raise the wall of taller forms. The "knuckle" (the first finger curled around into a "C" shape) of the right hand is underneath, and lifts the bulge up the wall as the wheel rotates fairly swiftly. This lift can be repeated until the clay wall reaches its desired height, but the clay can become weak if it is over worked. As the height of the wall increases then the speed of the wheel turning should be reduced.

method 6
In this process the rib is used to lift the wall. It replaces the fingers or knuckle on the outside wall of the pot. The left fingers are still pushing out a bulge of clay on the inside to the outside, but the rib is used under this bulge to push it upward to thin the walls. This is quite a difficult skill to learn. However, it does form a very strong, consolidated wall, making it a popular technique for throwing plant pots. Using the rib also means the outside of the pot does not need to be lubricated with water.

Throwing a simple cylinder

The following few pages illustrate the logical progression from ball of clay to cylinder. The cylinder is the basis for most upright forms, such as vases and jugs, and to master it will give a firm foundation for the beginner to work on.

Repetition is the best way to learn new skills; repeating an exercise shows you where you went wrong and the improvements you make as time goes by. A lot is written about forming bad habits early on as a beginner, but there are

1 **2** **3**

Center the clay on the wheel by cupping the hands around the ball and squeezing inward while exerting a downward pressure with the thumbs on the top of the clay (see pages 20–21). This two-way squeezing action forces the clay into a perfectly round, flattened cylinder of revolving clay. Remember to keep the forearms resting on the wheel tray and the elbows tucked into the side of the body. Lubricate the hands and clay with water as required. If the clay is uneven, use the coning up method of centering to even it out.

Now open the clay. Make sure the arms are locked in a strong position and the clay is well lubricated. Cup the hands around the swiftly revolving clay and push the thumb of the right hand directly into the center of the clay, down to about ¼ inch (6mm) from the wheel head, still supporting the wall of clay on the outside with the left hand. Keep the thumb directly in the middle until the correct depth is achieved (if it is off-center a hill of clay may form). Take the thumb out to check the depth. Try not to use too much water at this stage; if the hole fills with water it will be difficult to see what is happening.

Use the thumb to open and widen the hole. Continue to cup the clay with the hands. Do not use too much inward pressure, as it will prevent the clay from being forced out. The right thumb inside the opening slowly and steadily pushes the clay wall outward; any sudden movements may cause the clay to be knocked off-center. Keep the thumb at a fixed height as it moves out to form a smooth, flat base. Run the fingers back and forth over the base to consolidate the clay, making it less susceptible to cracking. The base should be finished now, as it will be difficult to get to when the walls have been formed. Initially it is easier to make low, wide cylinders that are less likely to wobble than taller forms. You can increase the height with subsequent attempts.

The inside base is at its final width.

The thumb widens the opening.

Both hands support the wall as it is formed.

The walls are thick and ready for thinning.

The base is flat and smooth.

The pin is pushed through the base while a finger is placed on the base.

A pin on a stick is used to measure the depth of the base.

When the pin is removed the finger is held in place on it and the depth can clearly be seen.

no hard and fast rules. If you get the result you want through methods you've developed yourself—good. However, the beginner should practice using the same weight of clay so that improvements in height and shape will be obvious. When improvements can clearly be seen you will feel motivated to carry on, and will retain more information for your next session at the wheel.

4 Carry out the first lift of the clay wall. Place the thumb of the left hand at the base of the pot on the outside and push it lightly inward to create a slight hollow. Curl the fingers of the left hand over the rim of the pot and place them on the inside. Rest the right hand on top of the left to give extra support. Squeeze the fingers of the left hand on the inside against the thumb on the outside to thin the clay wall slightly. Hold this grip as the fingers and thumb rise up the clay wall together. Less pressure is required as the wall increases in height because there is less clay to be thinned. Lightly rest part of the right hand on the rim of the rising wall to consolidate and compact it slightly so it doesn't become too uneven as thinning continues.

5 As the left hand rises, push it inward to narrow the cylinder slightly. Do not let the clay spread out as the wall is thinned; the clay naturally wants to widen due to the centrifugal force throwing it outward. As the left hand pushes inward, rest the right hand on the rim to help prevent it from spreading out too much. It is much easier to control a cylinder that is slightly narrower at the rim than the base, and it is easier to widen the rim later, rather than try to make it narrower. Use the raising and thinning action all the way up to the rim of the pot, but leave the rim slightly thicker than the walls. Try to keep the walls of an even thickness during the whole lifting process. With practice, this lifting action will only need to be done once, but initially a couple of lifts will be required.

6 A knuckle lift is now used to heighten and thin the wall further. With the left fingers still on the inside of the pot, push out a slight bulge at the base of the pot. Place the knuckle of the right hand under the bulge on the outside. Use the knuckle to slowly push the bulge up the wall of the pot. The wheel should be traveling a little slower at this stage. The fingers on the inside rise up the wall and continue to push out the bulge just ahead of the rising knuckle. This action squeezes and raises the walls of the pot, and this should be one continuous action from the base of the pot to the rim. Keep the upward movement of the hands slower than the revolution of the wheel to ensure a smooth, even lift. A series of neat throwing rings will be formed on the outside of the pot wall.

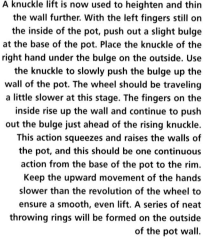

The thumb of the left hand is on the outside of the pot pushing inward and upward.

The right hand supports the left and consolidates the rim of the pot.

The left fingers squeeze the clay from the inside and thin the walls.

The walls are kept of an even thickness during lifting.

The base is at right angles to the wall.

Repeat the knuckle lift two or three times. Until your confidence builds up and the clay is more forcibly lifted, you may need to use more lifts. Try not to use too many lifts as this weakens and tires the clay and may cause it to collapse. If anything goes wrong, just start again with another ball of clay and try to correct your mistakes as you go along. It is a bad idea to try to rescue a collapsing pot, as this will only make subsequent shaping and forming more difficult. When they get nearer the top of the pot, the thumbs of both hands can be linked together to create more stability, especially when the height of the pot causes the left arm to leave the support of the wheel tray.

The cylinder has now reached its full height. A series of evenly spaced throwing rings can be seen on the surface. If the lifting had been uneven the rings would vary in size. The rim of the pot has been left slightly thicker than the walls, giving a neat, finished appearance to the pot. Use the little finger of the right hand to smooth the rim, applying just a little pressure, while supporting the wall with the left fingers on the inside and the left thumb on the outside. Some potters use a piece of leather to smooth the rim.

Use a triangular turning tool or throwing rib to create a bevel under the base of the cylinder. This bevel has a number of purposes. It creates an undercut to the base, which will guide the cutting wire under the pot neatly, and also gives the form a visible lift by removing a little weight from the base. Finally, the bevel gives a point to glaze to later. Place both hands on the tool and rest the forearms on the wheel tray. It is very important to keep the hands steady at this late stage. Place the tool at the base of the pot at an angle and slowly remove small amounts of clay as the wheel slowly rotates. It may be necessary to stop and clean the tool as it becomes clogged with wet clay.

Near the rim of the pot, the left thumb rests on the right hand to hinge the two together and add extra stability.

The left arm has had to move away from the support of the wheel tray.

The left fingers push out a bulge ahead of the knuckle.

The right knuckle lifts the clay upward and pushes it inward.

The walls are starting to thin evenly.

The rim is smoothed using the side of the little finger.

The cylinder is at its full height.

The wall is supported by the gripping action of the thumb and fingers of the left hand.

The walls are of an even thickness, though a little extra weight is left in the rim.

The base and walls of this cylinder are of the same thickness.

The evenly spaced throwing rings can clearly be seen on the inside of the cylinder.

The pot could be considered finished if you want the throwing rings to be a feature, as they often are in handmade pottery. Alternatively, the walls can be smoothed and have their strength increased using a throwing rib. With the right hand, place the rib against the base of the pot. Anchor the right arm to the edge of the wheel tray to hold it as steady as possible. Position the fingers of the left hand inside the pot and use them to gently push the clay against the rib on the outside. When using a rib you do not get any feedback through the fingers about how thin the wall is or how much pressure is being exerted, so complete this process cautiously until it becomes second nature. Push the rib slightly inward as it is pushed from within. Make sure the rib and fingers travel slowly, simultaneously, and evenly up the wall to the rim. Do not use water on the outside of the pot. The rib actually removes water and slurry from the walls of the pot, creating a dry, strong surface.

The pot is now finished. Use a sponge to remove water from the inside while the wheel is rotating slowly. If the cylinder is very narrow you may need to use a sponge on a stick to avoid distorting the walls. The pot now needs to be removed from the wheel. Hold a cutting wire taut between both hands. Use the first finger of each hand to hold the wire as tight and as flat to the wheel head as possible. Pass the wire under the base of the pot, pulling it toward you while keeping it taut. The wire has a tendency to rise up in the middle as it passes under the pot and cut through a thin base if it is not held as flat and as tight as possible. Pass the wire under the pot a couple of times to ensure it has been cut free and does not re-adhere to the wheel.

Dry your hands, then place them around the body of the cylinder. Do not squeeze the clay too much in one place. The dry fingers should stick to the still-wet surface of the clay to give a good grip. If they slide off, either the pot wall or the hands are too wet. Lift the pot cleanly upward away from the wheel. Use only enough pressure to lift, and do not squeeze inward. If the pot seems firmly stuck to the wheel, wire it again. This process takes a bit of practice. Alternatively you can throw directly onto a wooden bat (see page 35). Place the pot on a dry board to dry out. If the pot has become oval during the removal from the wheel, place the hands on the opposite sides from the way you lifted it and squeeze slightly inward. This should correct any unevenness in the roundness of the form.

Tips for success

- Use as much water as you need to prevent your hands from catching on the clay, but do not let it gather in the base of the pot, and be sure to remove it with a sponge if this happens. Some books advise using as little water as possible, but this is not always necessary, as commercially available clays are not likely to collapse from soaking up too much water during throwing. Clays sold as throwing clays are robust and prepared especially for ease of use.
- Use well-kneaded clay (see pages 16–17). Nothing hinders the even throwing of cylinders more than uneven clay. You can become disheartened if clay will not center, or the walls of the cylinder do not thin evenly. These conditions are often due to badly prepared, uneven, air-filled clay rather than the throwing technique.
- Be prepared to try and try again. It is a cliché, but practice makes perfect. Developing throwing skills takes some determination and a desire to improve.

Cylinder problems

While learning to throw, many things can go wrong and cause a pot failure. The clay can always be reclaimed or rekneaded when this happens (see pages 14 and 16–17), but before you do this, cut the pot in half to see if the reason for collapse is obvious. If you can see your mistake you can take measures to avoid repeating it. You can also see how you are progressing and how even the pot wall is. When learning, it is actually a good idea to throw clay to its limit and see where the point of collapse is. This will help you to set the parameters clearly in your mind so you know when a shape is becoming beyond control. Here are some of the most common problems encountered while throwing a basic cylinder.

This cylinder is typical of a beginner's pot. It is centered and round, but the clay wall has been left very heavy at the base. The clay in the walls has not been sufficiently thinned. This is a good pot but could be further refined to make an excellent and much taller cylinder. This amount of clay could be turned away when the pot reaches the leather-hard stage (see page 119), but it would be more efficient to try and use it to create a taller cylinder during the throwing process.

The clay here was not centered properly before opening. This has caused the pot walls to be thicker on one side of the pot. During the thinning process, the one side has produced a taller wall, so the whole rim of the pot undulates. This problem can also occur if the thumb was not placed centrally in the clay when it was opened. Alternatively, the pot wall has been squeezed unevenly or the hands were removed quickly or jerkily from the pot during the first lift. These are the most common reasons for a pot to fall off-center.

There are uneven spirals of clay on the walls of this cylinder. This is caused by the lift being performed too quickly. If the rising hands move up the pot wall quicker than the rotation of the wheel, this uneven spiraling will occur. Mild cases can be eliminated by using a throwing rib to compress the pot wall and spread the clay out more evenly. Similar spiral buckling can occur if the pot is thinned too much in one area. The pot can sometimes be rescued by strengthening the wall with a rib, but in most cases the wall will inevitably collapse.

This is a very extreme example of a pot wall made fatally weak by a thin area of clay that cannot support the weight above it. This can happen for a number of reasons. If the clay is squeezed for too long at one point and the fingers do not travel up the pot wall evenly, then one area can become thinner than the rest. A strong grip or the knuckle pushed into the rising wall too much at any given point could also cause this fault. The hands may have become too dry and snagged on the clay, tearing the clay wall. This kind of mistake is difficult to remedy and it would be easier to start again than correct it. Cutting the pot in half shows clearly where the fault has occurred, and examining it can help you understand why it has happened at this point, giving you the chance to re-examine your lifting technique.

General faults

Other faults, such as air bubbles and splitting or feathering of the clay, are usually caused by inadequate preparation of the clay. It cannot be stressed enough that clay should be well kneaded before throwing (see pages 16–17), otherwise failure is almost guaranteed. Even experienced potters find it difficult to work with clay that has not been kneaded sufficiently.

Learning from mistakes

Do not be afraid to make mistakes, it is all part of the learning process. Throwing is unique in that the material is never wasted and can be reused over and over again, so make mistakes and learn from them.

Cylinder refinements

Thankfully, there are two cylinder problems that can be easily remedied.

- If a cylinder has become too wide at the rim, then it can, if it has not widened too far, be collared in.

- If a rim is uneven it can be trimmed using a craft knife.

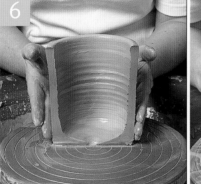

This cross-section shows that the pot wall has doubled back on itself and caused the pot to collapse downward. This can be caused by the pot filling with too much water and the base becoming saturated and unable to support its own weight. Alternatively, the wall may have been widened too much above the width of the base, causing the clay to fold over itself. This kind of fault can also happen when the clay is tired. If it has been on the wheel for a long time and overworked, it can become saturated with water or overthinned. One secret of throwing is knowing when to stop and start again. It is better to stop with an average pot than to try and over-refine a tired piece of clay, which may be on the verge of collapse.

This cylinder has a couple of faults. The base has a hole in it. The thumb was pushed down too far in the opening stages, a problem that was not detected earlier, perhaps due to the pot being full of water. This fault will not become apparent until all the water is removed or when the cutting wire cuts through the base during removal from the wheel. It is difficult to patch the base of a pot, as the added clay will not be as consolidated as the thrown clay and will inevitably crack during drying. It is also next to impossible to smooth the base because it is difficult to get the hand into a tall cylinder once the walls have been formed. Here there is also extra clay at the base of the walls. This should either have been left in the center of the base to make it thicker, or used in the walls to make the pot taller. During the first lift the fingers did not make a neat, right-angled corner or push the clay outward to be combined into the wall.

collaring in
Three points of pressure need to be applied to the pot in a triangle around it. Place the thumbs together at the back of the pot—the first point—and the fingers to either side at the front—the second and third points. Make sure the pot is well lubricated, as any snagging will easily tear the thinned wall. Squeeze, and gradually raise the hands up the side of the pot, pushing the clay evenly inward and narrowing the cylinder. The further down this process starts, the more likely the pot is to develop a wobble above the fingers. Narrowing the clay all in one go may buckle or fold the narrowing neck. Instead, use a couple of collars to achieve the narrowness required. This technique is also used to make bottles and narrow-necked vases, where the body of the pot is wider than the neck.

trimming a rim
Hold the knife in the right hand and place it lightly on the surface of the pot. Check it is positioned below the whole of the irregular rim by spinning the wheel slowly. Do not try just to remove the irregularity. It is best to remove a whole ring of clay to create an even rim. When you are happy with the position of the knife, slowly spin the wheel and press the knife onto the surface of the pot. It will eventually cut through the pot wall. Use the left hand to support the wall, but be careful not to cut your fingers as the knife cuts through it. When the cut is complete all the way around, the cut clay will sit on the rim of the pot. Swiftly move the cut clay upward by lifting it with the knife to remove it from the pot.

Throwing a simple bowl

When throwing bowls, the inside is more important than the outside. Bowls are rarely finished during the throwing process—they are usually turned later when they are firm enough to be handled (see pages 112–135).

Bowls are generally easier to throw than cylinders because the clay naturally wants to flare outward with the centrifugal pressure created by the revolving wheel. Smaller bowls are easy to control but centrifugal force tends

1

Center the clay, aiming to leave it low and flat (see pages 20–21). Use the side of the right hand to push the clay downward and displace it outward to create a very shallow dish. Use the left hand to support the widening form. This method of opening consolidates the base of the pot really well by pressing down and compacting it. If you want to turn a foot ring later, remember to leave the base much thicker so this can be formed. The side of the hand leaves a curved inner surface. Press the forearms onto the rim of the wheel tray to give them support. Lubricate the hands and clay whenever necessary.

2

The walls of the bowl are now formed. Place the thumb of the left hand under the wide, shallow rim of the bowl on the outside while the fingers curl over the rim of the bowl and sit on the inside. Rest the right hand on the rim of the bowl and over the left hand. Gently squeeze the left thumb and fingers together to thin the clay a little. The wheel should be traveling quite slowly during the formation of bowls, as any unevenness in the walls will be easily exaggerated if the wheel is spinning too fast. Use the side of the right hand to consolidate the clay at the rim and stop the clay widening out too much of its own accord.

3

Draw the left fingers and thumb outward and upward in one sweeping movement. Do not try to use up all the clay in one go, a couple of lifts are better than one. Try not to squeeze the clay too much at the base, since this may cause a weak point. The wall of the bowl should be raised up more than it is widened because it is easier to make the bowl wider later in the forming process, and almost impossible to make it narrower. The inside profile should be a continuous curve from rim to rim. Try to avoid a bump or right angle forming where the base turns into the wall. This change of direction should not be obvious; the inside of the bowl should be perfectly concave.

4

A knuckle lift now raises the wall of the pot further. Place the knuckle of the right hand a little way up from the base on the outside. Rather than push out a bulge for the knuckle to start under, simply press the clay outward with the left fingers, just ahead of the rising knuckle. As the knuckle progresses up the wall, more of a bulge is forced outward. Allow the clay to flare out slightly, but make sure the wall is also lifted, otherwise it may become too wide too quickly. Leave the rim of the bowl a little heavier to give a neat, strong finish to the bowl. Some potters prefer to use the fingers of the right hand on the outside of the pot rather than using the knuckle. You can use whichever method you are most comfortable with.

The right hand supports the left and consolidates the rim of the revolving clay wall.

The forearms rest on the wheel tray for support.

The thumb of the left hand is on the outside of the pot and the fingers are on the inside, ready to squeeze the clay upward and outward.

The right hand prevents the clay from widening too much.

The fingers and thumb of the left hand squeeze the clay upward and slightly outward.

The walls are starting to thin evenly.

The inside profile of the bowl is a sweeping curve from rim to rim.

to work against you as the forms become larger, so start small, and master the techniques before moving on to larger bowls.

Foot rings

To create deep, decorative foot rings, the base needs to be left thicker when opening and throwing. Check the depth with a pin to make sure you leave enough clay.

Bowl problems

Bowls can be easily knocked off-center by a sudden hand movement, especially if the clay is too dry or has been stretched too thinly. If the wheel is moving too swiftly, any problems will be quickly exaggerated.

The wall of the pot has only been lifted once. If you think the walls are still too thick, repeat the knuckle lift, but try not to overthin the walls as bowls soon become unstable and start to wobble. Smooth the rim of the bowl using the side of the little finger on the right hand and pinch the clay between the thumb and fingers of the left hand. A piece of leather can be used to smooth the rim if you prefer. The sides of this bowl are currently too straight, but it is easier to widen this than to make it narrower if you go too far too soon.

Widen the bowl to its finished shape using a throwing rib. The rib supports the wall over a larger area than either the knuckle or fingers could. At the base of the pot, place the rib on the pot on the outside, held in the right hand. Anchor the right arm to the edge of the wheel tray to hold it as steady as possible. Position the fingers of the left hand inside the pot, and use them to gently push the clay against the rib. Do not use any water to lubricate the outside of the pot, though some may be required on the inside to stop the fingers from snagging. While shaping the wall, remember it is the inside profile that needs to be perfect, make sure you maintain a smooth curve from rim to rim.

Many potters use a curved rib to create the inside curve. Lubricate the outside and support it with the fingers of the left hand. Press the curved rib onto the inner surface to smooth it and push any bumps or irregularities into the wall of the pot. This should be done with great care. Too much downward pressure may distort or widen the form too much. The downward pressure of the rib should be met with equal pressure from the fingers underneath. Using a rib smooths the inner surface into a perfect curve. If you can control the inner profile with just the fingers, it is not always necessary to use a rib. The bowl is now finished and can be removed from the wheel.

This cross-section shows a bowl that has been made fatally weak and has collapsed over its base. This can happen for a number of reasons. The bowl could have been made too wide for its base, or not enough clay was left at the base to support the widening wall. The clay may have become saturated with water left to gather in the base of the pot for too long, causing the clay to flop. The base of this bowl is also too flat and lumpy. The inside profile is not a smooth flowing curve. If this bowl had not collapsed over the base, it would probably still have slumped a little. We can tell this by the appearance of a raised ring of clay in the wall on the inside of the pot, interrupting the inside curved profile. This is something that often happens when you are beginning to make bowls and it is only with practice that problems like this can be overcome and eliminated.

The finished bowl has a smooth, flowing inner curve from rim to rim.

The rim is left a little heavier to give a strong, neat finish to the bowl.

The walls are of an even thickness, only tapering slightly toward the rim.

There is extra clay at the base of the wall on the outside. This has helped to support the wall during throwing and will be removed during turning.

Throwing from a hump

This technique is not widely used today, but it does have its advantages and it is useful to know how to do it. Small forms are thrown from a large piece of roughly centered clay.

Bowls

Throwing from the hump is an excellent way to make bowls at speed, without the need to measure out lots of small balls of clay. Once a bowl has been made, another lump can be centered and thrown immediately.

1 Place a large piece of well-kneaded clay (see pages 16–17) on the wheel. Roughly center it so that it does not wobble too much (see pages 20–21). It is not necessary to completely center the whole mass, as only the very top piece of clay will be used each time. Cup the hands around a section of clay at the top of the mass, about as much as 8 oz (250g). This lump needs to be centered properly. Squeeze the clay with the cupped hands and exert downward pressure with the thumbs on top of the clay. Rest the forearms on the wheel tray to help keep the hands still.

2 Open the centered piece of clay using the thumb of the right hand. Make sure the arms are locked in a strong position and the clay is well lubricated. Cup the hands around the swiftly revolving clay and push the thumb of the right hand directly into the center. It is difficult to judge the depth of the hole, as there is no base to relate to or push a pin into. Feeling for the base comes with practice and you will eventually know instinctively when it is the right depth. Use the fingers of the right hand to push a groove in the hump on the outside below the base of the pot. This will be the cut-off point later.

3 Form the walls of the bowl. Place the left thumb at the base of the pot on the outside and curl the left fingers over and inside the bowl. Position the right hand over the left to support it. Squeeze the clay between the thumb and fingers of the left hand to thin the wall. Hold this grip as the thumb and fingers travel up the wall of revolving clay to heighten it. Let the side of the right hand consolidate the rim of the pot while the whole hand keeps the left hand steady as it moves upward and away from the support of the wheel tray. Lubricate the bowl with water as needed.

4 Just one lift should be sufficient for such a small bowl, but you may need to lift it further. The base of the bowl is now formed. This base has a roll foot because it is easier to cut a straight line under a bevel, and the resulting bowl will have a more finished appearance. Bowls made in this way are quite organic and less likely to need turning later. One advantage of this method of making bowls is that the underside of the bowl profile can be more clearly seen. When thrown directly on the wheel, you have to get your eyes down to the level of the wheel head to see the outside profile.

5 To cut the bowl from the hump, hold a cutting wire taut and pass it through the clay, under the roll foot. It is difficult, at first, to judge the height of the wire as it cuts through. It is easiest if you start on the blind side and cut toward your body. Dry the hands and lift the bowl free of the hump. Grip the bowl at its base, using the middle fingers and the thumbs, and lightly grip the sides with the first fingers to stop the form distorting too much. Do not squeeze the clay; just lift it upward and place it on a dry board to dry. The fingerprints left in the roll foot may need to be smoothed away later when the clay has stiffened.

Lids

The main way in which throwing from the hump is used on a regular basis is to make lids. The underneath profile can be clearly seen, which is difficult when such a small form is made directly on the wheel head with small balls of clay.

Knobs

If you want a lid with enough clay in it to form a knob (see pages 154–157), then a deeper stem needs to be cut off from the hump. Simply create the cut-off point about 1 inch (2.5cm) lower down on the hump.

1 Place a large piece of well-kneaded clay (see pages 16–17) on the wheel. Roughly center it so that it does not wobble too much (see pages 20–21). It is not necessary to completely center the whole mass, as only the very top piece of clay will be used. It is difficult initially to know how much clay is needed to make a specific size of lid; again this comes with practice. Take a small lump of clay at the top of the hump and center it by squeezing it between cupped hands and exerting downward pressure with the thumbs on top of the clay. Rest the forearms on the wheel tray to help keep the hands still. The wheel should be traveling fairly swiftly throughout this process.

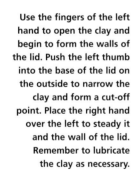

2 Use the fingers of the left hand to open the clay and begin to form the walls of the lid. Push the left thumb into the base of the lid on the outside to narrow the clay and form a cut-off point. Place the right hand over the left to steady it and the wall of the lid. Remember to lubricate the clay as necessary.

3 Press the little finger of the right hand into the wall on the outside to form the lip of the lid: this creates a flange and ledge. Use a few fingers of the left hand inside the pot to support the wall and one finger on the outside to support the right little finger. Squeeze the clay in, using the fingers and thumb to thin the wall of the hump below the lid a little. This gives a point from which to wire the lid from the hump.

4 Hold a cutting wire taut between the two hands and draw it toward you through the clay under the lid at the thinned point previously formed. Try to keep the wire as flat and level as possible. It does not matter too much if it is a bit crooked, as the lid will probably be turned later (see pages 138–145).

5 Remove the lid from the hump with clean, dry hands. Grip the lid around its base and lift it sharply upward. Place it on a clean dry board until it is ready to turn.

Repetition throwing

At some stage in your path as a potter you will undoubtedly be asked to make a set of mugs or bowls almost identical in size and shape. Some potters think the idea of creating two identical forms is a waste of time and goes against the idea of the handmade form. Others believe that being able to repeat a good form over and over again is a necessary part of the potter's repertoire. We will leave you to develop your own philosophy on this point, and supply you with the information you need to repeat a form over and over again.

Weigh up a few balls of clay of identical weight. Place them on or near the wheel. Throw a form that you wish to repeat, here a bowl (see pages 30–31). When you are happy with the bowl and it has been completely finished, set up the measuring gauge. These can be purchased from most ceramic suppliers, or you can make your own. This one has a metal post with another metal rod attached to it. The rod can be moved in and out and so can be adjusted to the exact width and height of the bowl. It is also possible to stick a rod into a ball of clay and use this as a marker, but this is easily knocked or the measurement can change as the clay ball dries. Position the gauge so that the end of the rod almost touches the rim of the bowl. Remove the bowl from the wheel but leave the gauge in position.

Throw another a bowl. The measuring gauge indicates the height and width of the rim of the pot and a point to aim to when making the next bowl.

The rim of the second bowl is now the same width and height as the first. The measuring gauge cannot, however, tell you any of the other measurements at any other point on the curve of the bowl. These details are replicated simply by observing the first bowl and trying to recreate them. More complicated measuring sticks that can be set to three different points on the surface of a form can be purchased. These are cumbersome and unnecessary and do detract from the handmade philosophy. The shape of the form can be repeated just by the one measurement and the judgment of the eye.

Overdoing it

It is a worthwhile exercise to do some repetition throwing. Repeating an action 10 or 12 times helps to increase your understanding of how a shape is formed and it gets easier and quicker the more often it is repeated. However, it can also soon become boring and unhelpful if hundreds of identical forms are created, so do not over labor the point of repetition throwing—unless, of course, you receive an order for 100 identical bowls.

Throwing a bat

There are many forms that can be created on the wheel that are difficult to remove when they are wet and the clay is still flexible, such as large bowls, or forms that have such flat bases that removing them from the wheel would be almost impossible. In these instances the pot can be made on a removable wooden bat. Expensive locating bats and bat rings can be purchased to fit onto the wheel head and, in turn, fit the bat to, but there is a cheaper alternative that uses just a pad of clay.

1 Center a ball of clay on the wheel head (see pages 20–21). Use the side and heel of the hand to push down on the clay and force it outward. Keep the pressure even as the clay is flattened. The wheel should be turning swiftly, and the hands and clay should be kept well lubricated.

2 Continue to force the clay outward using the side of the hand. A wall of clay will form in front of the hand. Continue to push this outward until you run out of clay and the base is completely flat.

3 Smooth the base flat with your fingers, and even out any irregularities. Ideally the whole of the wheel head should be covered with a pad of clay about ½ inch (1.5cm) thick. If you find the clay difficult to flatten, press down on a throwing rib that will cover a wider surface area than the fingers can.

4 Press the fingers down into the flat clay to create a series of concentric rings. These indentations will create pockets for air to be trapped in that will create suction with the wet clay when the wooden bat is placed on top, thus holding it in position.

5 Place a wooden bat centrally on the clay pad. Secure it in position by striking the bat firmly in the middle with a clenched fist. The sticky clay and suction will hold the wooden bat in place while the pot is formed on top of it. To check it is stuck, push it slightly to ensure it does not move. When the pot is finished the bat should be eased up from the pad slowly. Try not to jerk the bat, as this may distort the newly formed, wet pot. If you find the bat difficult to remove, use a strong metal tool to lever it off slowly. Subsequent bats that are used will become easier to remove as the clay pad starts to dry a little. If it becomes too dry, wet it again and redefine the suction rings.

Economy alternatives

Bats can be obtained from pottery suppliers, but it is usually cheaper to get them cut to size at your local timber store. The best material to make wooden bats from is marine plywood. This is designed, as the name suggests, for making boats, so it is resistant to warping when wet. Other woods may, over time, absorb moisture and begin to bend or buckle.

A heavy rim gives a definite finish to the pot. This also decreases the chance of the rim distorting and causing the pot to become oval, as it may if it were very thin.

The cylinder shape of a straight vase makes it the perfect stepping stone to other projects.

Straight Vase

The walls are of even thickness. It is a good idea to practice getting them as even as possible.

The base is left slightly thicker than the walls. The extra weight gives more stability to the pot.

This cone is an elegant shape but could be unstable. If used for flowers, an uneven arrangement could result in the pot being easily knocked over. Thickening the base will assist with stability.

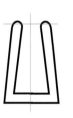

An inverted cone is a contemporary shape and is very stable. If the base is too wide it could look heavy and badly proportioned. The height and width need to be considered to make this shape easy on the eye. The base is trimmed slightly straighter than the rest of the pot, giving it punctuation and a lift, and making it appear less solid.

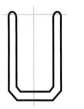

A very straight form with a rim as thick as its walls can look pure and minimalist when executed correctly. The base, however, needs to be tapered in, as even a very straight cylinder will have the illusion of looking wider at the base.

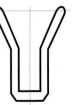

A cylindrical element can be used with other shapes to create composite forms. An interesting shape like this could be used as a vase or just as a sculptural object.

This simple shape is the starting point for most curved pots and is actually quite difficult to achieve, as you need plenty of concentration and control over the clay to successfully form straight sides. You may find it useful to start with smaller amounts of clay and then increase later.

A straight vase can be used for flowers, paintbrushes, and utensils, as well as having many other uses, so consideration has to be given to stability by way of the thickness of the base.

This vase is made using 4 lb (1.8kg) of clay, which should make a vase that is approximately 10 inches (25cm) high and 5 inches (13cm) wide when freshly made and still wet.

KEY

◄ Pulling, lifting, and shaping movements

◄ Pushing, thickening, and supporting movements

Once you have centered the clay (see pages 20–21), with the wheel turning quickly press the thumb of your right hand into the center of the clay, remembering to leave a fairly thick base. Use a pin to test the thickness if you find it difficult to guess. While your left hand supports the clay, use the thumb of your right hand to open out the clay and make it as wide now as it will be in the finished pot. Lubricate the clay with water as often as needed, but try not to let it collect in the base, as this will weaken it during throwing.

Use the tips of your fingers to consolidate the base of your pot by pressing down on the newly formed base to compress the clay. This will prevent it from cracking during drying and firing.

You now need to lift and squeeze the clay. Place the thumb of your left hand at the base of the pot on the outside and place the fingers of the same hand inside it. Position your right hand on the rim of the pot and over the left hand to provide support. Squeeze the thumb and fingers of your left hand together slightly at the base of the pot. Holding this position, slowly bring your left hand up the side of the pot, squeezing as you continue upward.

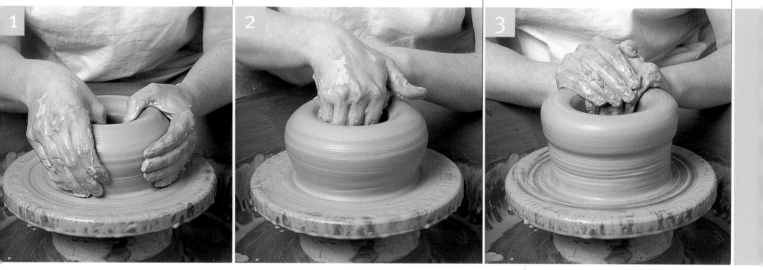

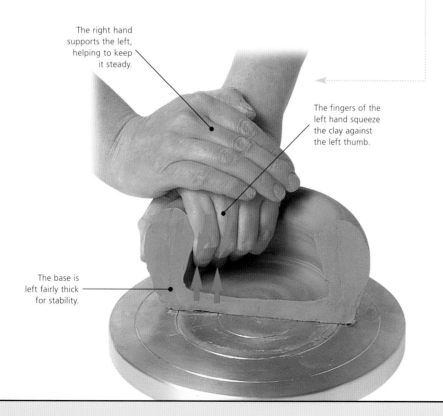

The right hand supports the left, helping to keep it steady.

The fingers of the left hand squeeze the clay against the left thumb.

The base is left fairly thick for stability.

Continue to squeeze the clay upward. To ensure an even lift keep the vertical movement of the hands slower than the revolving wheel. This helps keep the walls of even thickness; moving too quickly upward would create uneven spirals in the clay. As the clay wall increases in height the amount of clay between the thumb and fingers decreases, so less pressure is needed to squeeze it. The finished pot has a heavy rim, so leave a band of clay to form this.

Now you need to thin the walls of the pot further. Support the clay wall on the inside with your left hand as the fingers of the right hand push into the base of the pot against your fingers on the inside. This creates a bulge of clay near the base.

Place the knuckle of the right hand under this bulge and keep the left hand inside the pot, inside the bulge just above the knuckle of the right hand on the outside. With your arms firmly tucked into your body to help hold them still, slowly lift the bulge of clay up the pot against the fingers of the left hand inside the pot. The vertical movement of the hands should be slower than the revolution of the wheel. You should clearly see the bulge working its way up the pot.

The fingers travel up the clay wall, continuing to squeeze as they go.

The clay decreases in thickness as the height of the pot increases.

The wall is thinning evenly. The pressure of the squeeze should be reduced as the form becomes taller.

The fingers of the left hand force out a bulge as the right knuckle squeezes the clay inward, thinning it and preventing it from flaring outward.

The clay should be forced slightly inward to stop it flaring outward.

Some excess clay is left at the wheel head. This will be removed later.

Do not let your hands move outward as they move up. The clay naturally wants to move out as it spins, so apply more pressure on the outside as you lift upward to push the clay in slightly. If the pot does become too wide, you may have to collar it in slightly by placing both hands on the outside and applying gentle pressure while moving your hands upward to push the clay back into a straight cylinder. As you approach the top of the pot, remember to leave a band of clay with which to form the heavier rim.

Repeat the process of creating a bulge at the base and using the knuckle of the right hand and the fingers of the left hand to lift and squeeze the clay upward, thinning it until the desired height is achieved. Do not, however, overwork the clay. Ideally, three lifts at most should be used, but more may be required until you become more experienced. Do not be too disappointed if you cannot achieve the height; as long as the shape is correct the rest will come with practice. Remember to lubricate the hands and clay between lifts, and sponge out excess water that collects inside the pot.

The pot is now at full height. Use a throwing rib to scrape excess clay away from the wheel head by holding the rib against the base of the vase, and against the surface of the wheel. Throwing rings in the wall of the pot can be clearly seen. The pot at this stage could be considered finished if the ribbed surface is what you want to achieve. It does make a clear statement about how the pot was formed on the potter's wheel.

An excess band of clay is left at the lip to form the rim of the pot later.

The hands should be held very steady. Tucking your arms into your body will help with stability.

The walls are kept at even thickness as the height increases.

A throwing rib can be used to smooth the outside of the pot. Support the clay on the inside with your left hand and push it against the rib to consolidate the clay walls. Using a rib also removes any excess slurry that may have formed on the outside walls of the pot during the forming process. At this stage only the inside should be lubricated with water, because the rib does not snag on the clay like the fingers do.

Use the point of the throwing rib at an angle to undercut the base of the pot, holding the flat edge of the rib on the spinning wheel and pushing it slightly under the base of the pot to remove a sliver of clay. This removes any excess weight and improves the finished shape giving a visual lift to the form. It also provides a clean bevel that makes wiring the pot off the wheel head easier. Clean out all the water on the inside of the pot with a sponge.

Place two lines on the pot as guidelines for decoration. It is easier to do this now while the pot is centered on the wheel, rather than later when it has been removed. Hold the corner of the rib against the pot as it rotates slowly to mark the first line. Repeat to mark a second line, about 1½ inches (4cm) below the first.

Use a wire to cut the pot from the wheel head. Keep the wire taut and completely flat with the wheel head. Pulling the wire toward you is easiest. Dry your hands on a towel, place them around the pot, and lift upward. The pot should easily come away from the wheel. If it is still stuck, wire it again and try once more. Place the pot on a dry wooden bat to dry.

The rim is smoothed with the first finger of the right hand as the shape is controlled by the grip of the left-hand thumb and fingers.

The walls have been smoothed by a throwing rib on the outside, but the throwing rings can still be seen clearly on the inside.

The beveled base of this pot has not yet been formed, but you can see how it will remove some excess clay from the base of the vessel.

Allow the vase to dry for about three hours or until the rim has started to "go off," that is to say has started to stiffen but still has some flexibility in it. This is known as the "leather hard" stage, at which point it is possible to cut a design into the clay. The base of the pot will still be fairly wet, so take care not to distort it. Use a sharp craft knife to cut shapes from the outside of the pot, between the two guidelines marked earlier. For personalized gifts, it is possible to cut names into the pattern.

This vase does not need turning, unless you feel the profile is not straight enough or you have left the base too thick. Any turning would need to be done before the decoration was cut, as this makes the pot very fragile. The design on this vase is loosely based on an abstracted Celtic knot, but you can, of course, personalize the vase with your own design, or leave it plain.

The neck of the vase is narrower than the base, thus giving more stability. This is a good place to add a decorative touch such as a groove.

Curved forms are often easier to create than straight ones, and the eye is less critical of the finished shape.

Curved Vase

This is a good shape because the base of the pot is wider than the neck, making the whole vase stable. The form is pleasing to the eye since the widest part of the pot, the belly, is above the halfway line. Above the belly the shoulder of the pot tapers to the neck.

Vessels of this shape are elegant but can be unstable when filled with large flower arrangements. Thickening the base of such a pot would assist stability, but the pot could still be easily knocked over.

A beaker vase is a common shape. Although the neck is wider than the base, the base is still wide enough to be stable. Again, a slightly thicker base helps by adding more weight.

This vase shows that the addition of a wide and deep foot can create more stability without losing the appearance of being very narrow at the base. The foot also adds an interesting feature, and gives the pot a visible lift to its form.

Vases, jars and storage vessels have long been essential elements of domestic life. When setting out to design and create a pottery vase, it pays to consider what its end use will be. If it is to have a practical purpose, considerations such as stability and proportion need to be addressed. For a purely decorative piece, any shape can be considered.

All thrown vases start in the form of a basic thrown cylinder. From this cylinder any number of styles and shapes can be created. The curved vase illustrated here is a traditional shape, incorporating most of the basic throwing techniques needed to create other shapes.

This vase was made using 2 lb (900g) of clay which should make a vase that is approximately 8 inches (20cm) high and 4 inches (10cm) wide when freshly made and still wet.

KEY

Pulling, lifting, and shaping movements

Pushing, thickening, and supporting movements

The walls are of an even thickness, only tapering slightly toward the neck. This is normal in a handmade vessel.

The base is left slightly thicker than the walls, and the extra weight increases stability.

Once you have centered the clay (see pages 20–21), use the thumb of your right hand to open it out, while your left hand supports the revolving clay. Lubricate the clay with water but try not to use too much as excess can soak in and cause the pot to collapse. With the wheel turning quickly, press the right thumb firmly into the center of the clay. Push the thumb down until the correct base depth is achieved. If you are unsure about this check the depth of the base with a pin. Begin to push the thumb outward to widen the hole.

Next you need to lift and squeeze the clay. Tuck your elbows into the side of your body and rest your forearms on the lip of the wheel tray. This helps to lock your hands in position. Place the thumb of your left hand at the base of the pot on the outside and the fingers of this hand inside the pot. Place your right hand on top to provide support. Squeeze the thumb and fingers of your left hand together with a firm and even pressure. Slowly bring your fingers up the side of the pot, squeezing as you continue upward.

Push the clay inward as you move upward to prevent the clay trying to move out as it spins. To ensure an even lift, keep the vertical movement of the hands slower than the revolving wheel. At this stage the wheel should still be turning quite swiftly. As the clay walls increase in height, the amount of clay between the thumb and fingers decreases and so less pressure is needed to squeeze the clay. Try not to make the rim of the pot too thin by over-squeezing the clay as you approach the top.

The right thumb pushes outward and downward, creating the base of the pot as well as widening the form.

The base of the right hand rests on the rim of the pot, compressing and consolidating the clay. It is also helping to prevent the clay moving out too much.

The left hand supports the clay wall.

The base is left quite thick for stability.

The left thumb, on the outside of the pot, should be just slightly higher than the fingertips of the left hand as the clay is squeezed and raised.

The walls of the pot should be of even thickness; to achieve this the pressure needs to be reduced as the form becomes taller.

Now thin the clay further. With the fingers of the left hand press out a slight bulge from inside the pot. Place the knuckle of the right hand underneath this bulge on the outside. The fingertips of the inside hand should be placed slightly above the knuckle to support the clay with gentle, even pressure. With your arms firmly tucked into your body to help hold your hands steady, slowly push the bulge upward. You should now see the bulge work its way easily up the pot right to the rim. Remember to lubricate the clay with water whenever it begins to dry out.

You have now reached the rim of the pot. To shape it, place the left thumb on the outside of the vase under the rim and curl the fingers over the top of the rim inside the vase. Support the left hand with the right hand on top. With your left thumb, gently push the clay inward to narrow the neck slightly, while your fingers support it from the inside. Gently squeeze the clay with your fingers and thumb; this will flare the rim out slightly. Repeating step 4, create a bulge to bring the vase to its full height. You may need to use a couple of lifts, but try not to make too many as it may tire the clay and make it difficult to control.

The pot at this stage should be slightly taller than the finished vase, because as shaping proceeds, some of the height will be lost. To begin shaping the vase, keep the same hand position, but this time use the fingertips of the left hand to push the clay walls gently outward. The wheel should now be revolving more slowly. As the body of the vase begins to swell, support the clay with the knuckle of the right hand to prevent it from widening too far. Continue to use just enough water to prevent your hands snagging on the clay as the pot takes shape.

The fingers on the inside force out a bulge in the clay wall that is pushed upward by the knuckle on the outside.

The fingers of the left hand on the inside of the pot are just above the knuckle of the right hand on the outside.

The walls are now thinner, but they still have an even thickness.

The neck of the pot at this stage has to be wide enough to get the left hand inside to shape the vase.

The fingers and thumb of the left hand push the neck inward slightly and begin to form the neck and rim of the vase.

The walls have been thinned by pressure applied when pulling up.

Use a throwing rib to create a smooth surface on the outside of the vase. During this process only lubricate the inside of the pot. Hold the rib in your right hand against the surface of the pot, angling it inward slightly toward the clay. Place the fingers of the left hand on the inside of the pot to support the clay. Starting at the bottom of the pot, very gently push the clay onto the rib. Continue all the way up the vessel to smooth the surface and remove finger marks and throwing rings made during the throwing process. This also removes excess water from the surface of the pot.

A decorative groove can be added to the base of the neck using the corner of the rib. Support the clay on the inside with the fingers of the left hand as you push the corner of the rib into the base of the neck on the outside. Do not push too hard as this may cut through the pot. The wheel should be revolving quite slowly at this stage.

To finish shaping the flared rim of the vase, use the little finger of the right hand on the outside and the fingers of the left hand on the inside. Gently squeeze the clay at the rim of the pot to thin it a little more, and flare the clay out to give a pleasant finish. This should be done with very gentle pressure so as not to tear the rim away from the pot.

The fingers of the left hand support the clay directly opposite the rib on the inside of the pot, moving up the pot as the rib moves up.

The left thumb helps support the clay on the outside as the rib cuts a small indent in the surface of the pot.

Remember not to press down too hard on the pot from above or it may collapse, and try to keep all movements controlled.

Using the rib compresses the clay, creating a stronger pot and giving a smoother surface on which to decorate later.

The left fingers must support the neck.

The rib follows the form of the pot.

The neck of the vase may now be too narrow to place your hand inside, so remove any excess water that may have gathered in the base of the pot using a sponge on a stick to avoid distorting the neck.

Remove excess clay on the wheel head by holding the flat edge of the throwing rib on the spinning wheel and pushing it slightly under the base of the pot, giving a bevel finish to the vase. This bevel provides a neat finish to the vase, a groove in which to guide the cutting wire, and a point to glaze to.

The neck is now slightly narrower than the base, which creates a more stable vase.

A decorative groove has been cut into the neck of the vase.

A sponge on a stick is used to remove water rather than a hand since it is less likely that you will touch the sides of the pot and distort the form. It is also useful if the neck is too thin for your hand to fit in.

The walls of the vase are of even thickness, tapering only slightly toward the neck.

Cut the pot from the wheel with a wire. Keep the wire taut and flat with the wheel head and pull it toward you. Once you have dried your hands, lift the pot off the wheel, placing your hands under the belly of the vase and lifting it smoothly upward. The pot should easily come away from the wheel. If it is still stuck, wire it once more and try again.

A vase made in this way needs no turning of the foot ring, unless you feel that you have left too much weight at the base, or you want to add extra features at a later stage. You can see how the beveled foot gives a visual lift to the pot and provides a line to glaze to. This prevents the glaze sticking the vase to the kiln shelf during firing. Applying different pressures and shaping to the form can create a variety of different vases. Be creative and invent your own forms. Alternatively, copying historical pots can be very rewarding.

This project creates three different objects from one simple cylinder form.

Mug, Jug & Oil Burner

This shape is known as a cooling tower. It is very cylindrical but is a nice shape to hold and drink from, and can be elongated or made more squat to create variations. A pouring lip can easily be made from the rim to make a matching jug.

A simple, straight-sided mug can be uninteresting, but with the addition of a quirky handle it is transformed. Straight forms are more difficult to create pouring lips from, as there is little extra clay from which to create them. Alternatively, a separate lip could be made and added later.

This contemporary cone shape is easy to throw because the clay naturally flares outward at the rim. It is fairly easy to create a pouring lip as the flaring rim provides enough clay, and the direction of the lip doesn't need to be changed.

The concentric rings of this elaborate shape can be formed using a throwing rib. A larger form could be created to make an interesting lemonade jug with perhaps six smaller mugs or beakers without handles to complete the set.

Mugs and jugs are everyday functional objects. The variety of shapes and forms seems to be inexhaustible, and they are an essential part of any potter's repertoire. Some mugs and cups, such as Eastern tea bowls, do not have handles, but the majority of drinking and pouring vessels do. Handles should be easy to pick up and comfortable in the hand.

The oil burner is a relatively new concept in the West. Water and a few drops of essential oils are warmed in a dish over a small candle, imparting aromatherapy benefits to the air. The distance between the candle and lid is very important, so that the oil burner does not smoke or heat the water too much.

The basic shape uses 12 oz (350g) of clay for a mug/jug approximately 4 inches (10cm) high and 4 inches (10cm) wide when still wet. The lid for the oil burner uses 7 oz (198g) of clay.

KEY

Pulling, lifting, and shaping movements

Pushing, thickening, and supporting movements

A rounded rim prevents chipping and is smooth to drink from.

A narrow neck provides a point to attach a handle to and is also decorative.

The walls are quite thin and of even thickness.

A curved inner and outer base gives a nice rounded form, which is comfortable to hold.

Once you have centered the clay (see pages 20–23), lubricate the hands well with water and push the thumb of the right hand into the revolving clay while supporting the wall from the outside with the left hand. The wheel should be moving quickly at this stage. Push the thumb down until the correct base depth is achieved. Test this with a pin to be sure. This is quite a small pot and the walls will be quite thin, so the base needs to be fairly thin also. Once the hole is created, push the thumb outward to widen it.

To lift and squeeze the clay, place the left thumb at the base of the outside of the pot and the fingers of the same hand on the inside. Use the right hand over the left to support it. Gently but firmly squeeze the fingers and thumb of the left hand together to thin the clay wall slightly. Rest the right hand on the rim of the pot, compressing the clay and preventing it from moving outward.

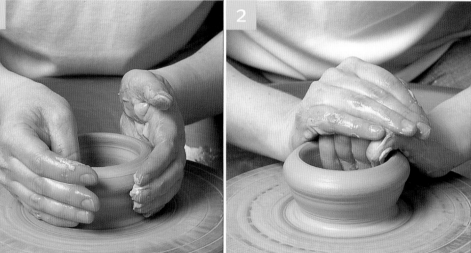

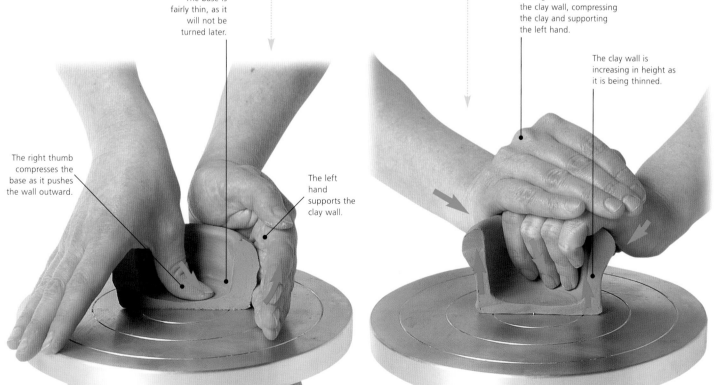

The base is fairly thin, as it will not be turned later.

The right thumb compresses the base as it pushes the wall outward.

The left hand supports the clay wall.

The right hand rests on the clay wall, compressing the clay and supporting the left hand.

The clay wall is increasing in height as it is being thinned.

Continue squeezing the clay gently upward between the left thumb and fingers. To ensure an even lift, keep the vertical movement of the hands slower than the revolving wheel. As the clay walls increase in height, the amount of pressure required to squeeze them is reduced because there is less clay to thin. Push gently inward as you approach the rim of the pot to prevent the clay from flaring outward.

Push a groove into the base of the pot with the little finger of the right hand. This narrows the base. Push out a bulge of clay from the inside with the left fingers above the little finger on the outside, ready for the lifting process. Support the rim of the pot with the left thumb on the outside.

Place the knuckle of the first finger of the right hand under the bulge of clay, then lift the bulge upward as the wheel rotates fairly quickly. Continue to push the clay out from the inside with the left fingers just ahead of the knuckle. Keep supporting the rim with the left thumb to prevent it from moving outward too much. Keep the hands lubricated, but mop out any excess water gathering in the pot.

One lift may be sufficient, but it may take two or three until this process is perfected. As the bulge travels to the rim of the pot, be careful not to oversqueeze and make the rim too thin. Use the fingers of the left hand to gently fold the rim over the knuckle to form a slightly flared rim. The rim should now be at its finished width, 4 inches (10cm) wide.

3

4

5

6

The fingers of the left hand are slightly above the knuckle of the right hand.

The left thumb supports the neck.

The walls are of even thickness.

The knuckle lifts the bulge in the clay wall upward.

The pot is now at full height.

The thumb and fingers of the left hand form the rim of the pot, flaring it outward.

The walls and base are of even thickness.

Use a throwing rib to remove any excess clay from the base of the pot at the wheel head by pressing it slightly into the base to create a bevel under it. This removes any excess clay that may have been left there during throwing.

Use the rib to smooth and support the outside walls of the pot as the left fingers on the inside push against the wall to swell the belly outward. This strengthens the clay wall and removes excess water. Smooth the flared neck of the pot with the rib by gently pushing the rim from the inside with the left fingers onto the curved side of the rib. You can narrow the neck slightly by pressing the rib inward, but make sure the left hand supports the clay on the inside. A sharp movement could distort the pot.

The basic mug shape is now complete. If you wish to form the mug into a jug or make the oil burner, leave it on the wheel. Otherwise, wire the pot off making sure the wire is taut and close to the wheel head. Pull the wire toward you to cut smoothly across. Place clean, dry hands around the belly of the pot and lift it cleanly upward to remove it from the wheel. Keep the pressure of the hands even so as not to distort it. If it is still stuck, wire once more and try again. Place the pot on a dry board.

To make a jug out of the basic mug shape without turning the wheel, use the thumb and first finger of the right hand to gently smooth an area of the rim flat. Very gently squeeze as you flatten to thin the clay a little. Gently pull the clay upward slightly to extend the height of this area of clay.

7

8

9

10

The thumb of the left hand supports the neck of the pot.

The rib is used to smooth the outside wall, shaping it and removing excess water and slurry.

The rib is held against the wheel head and gently pushed into the pot at the base, removing any excess clay there.

The rim of the pot is as wide as the belly.

The walls are of even thickness.

The fingers of the left hand push the clay against the rib.

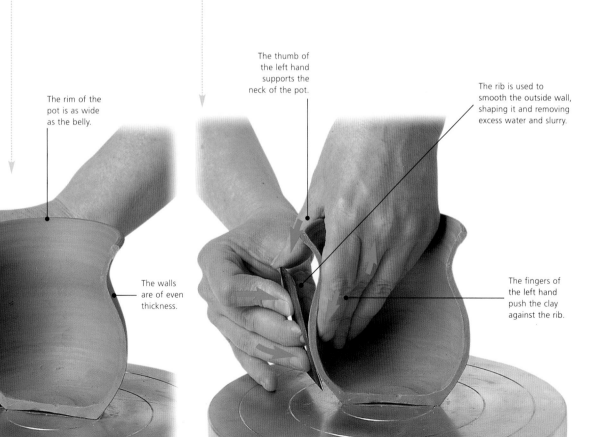

Place the left thumb on one side of the flattened area and the first finger of the left hand on the other side with the rest of the hand above the pot. Gently squeeze the thumb and finger in a little. Using the first finger of the right hand, begin to shape the pouring lip. The finger should be well lubricated and moved from side to side, gently easing the clay downward and bending the rim over to form the lip. This is quite difficult the first time you do it, but with practice you will become more confident.

To narrow the lip, gently squeeze it in with the finger and thumb of the right hand and push upward a little to define the shape. The jug is now finished. Wire the jug from the wheel head. Keep the wire taut and close to the wheel head as you pull it toward you, cutting smoothly across. With dry, clean hands, transfer it to a dry board. If the shape has been distorted during the forming of the pouring lip or the removal from the wheel, gently push the clay back into position.

The jug and mug each need to have a handle fitted. The same technique can be used for both. The pot needs to be dry enough not to distort when picked up, but still softer than leather hard, otherwise the handle will dry at a different rate and may crack or fall off. Use a craft knife to mark a small crosshatched area on the pot just below the neck. On the jug, this area also needs to be directly opposite the pouring lip. This forms a key for the handle to grip to. Dab a little slurry from the wheel tray onto this area.

Handles can be made in many different ways (see pages 148–153). This handle has been formed using an extruder into which a former, shaped in a grooved design, has been placed. Take a short length of this extrusion and push it onto the crosshatched area, smoothing the join with the thumb of the right hand. Make sure it is well stuck, and the handle join is blended into the pot.

11

12

13

14

The clay at the rim is smoothed downward by the first finger of the right hand, as it moves back and forth from side to side.

The clay rim is supported by the thumb and first finger of the left hand

Form the handle into a curve and attach it at the other end, just above the base of the pot, with more crosshatching and a little slurry. Do not pick the pot up by the handle until it is fired, as it will either bend or snap off. On the jug, check that the handle is opposite the lip. Look across the jug to the lip to check the alignment. To finish, smooth the base of the pot with your fingers or run a sponge around it to tidy up any marks or sharp edges. Do not overwet the pot or sponge the clay too much.

To make the oil burner, first make the basic mug shape. Measure the width of the rim so that when you throw the lid you can make sure it fits. Wire the pot off the wheel head. Place clean, dry hands around the belly of the pot and lift it cleanly upward to remove it from the wheel. Keep the pressure of the hands even so as not to distort the pot. If it is still stuck, wire once more. Place the pot on a dry board.

The lid is quite a small form to throw, so little pressure is needed to create it. Center the clay and push the right thumb into the center. Supporting the clay wall with the left hand, gently push the thumb outward, raising it slightly as you go, ensuring it is well lubricated. The base of the inside of the lid should be bowl shaped and curved. Use the right-hand fingers to press down on the base of the pot to consolidate and strengthen it, as it needs to be strong to take the heat of the burning candle.

Gently squeeze out the lid with the thumb of the left hand under the lip and the first finger on the top of the wall. The rest of the fingers of the left hand support the inner bowl. Push the clay over and outward to create the lip.

15

16

17

18

The right hand helps to hold the left hand steady.

The lip of the lid is formed from the heavy rim by squeezing the clay between the finger and thumb of the left hand.

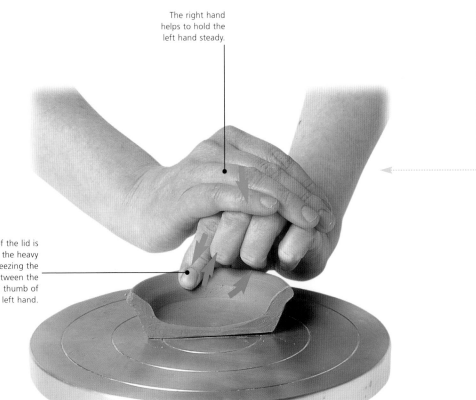

Use the finger of the right hand to smooth the newly formed rim as the left thumb supports it from underneath.

Remove excess clay from the wheel head using a throwing rib at an angle against the wheel head. Gently push the rib into the base of the lid to create a bevel to guide the cutting wire into.

Measure the width of the lid; ideally it should be ¼ inch (1.5cm) larger than the rim of the mug measured earlier. It looks better if it overhangs the pot and does not risk falling in. The bowl of the lid keeps it in place when finished. If the lid is not large enough, gently squeeze the rim out between the thumb and fingers of the left hand.

To remove the lid from the wheel, flood the wheel head with water and then wire the lid off. This will cause it to aquaplane and be easily pushed across the wheel onto the fingers of the right hand. Place it on a dry board to stiffen. When the lid has dried a little, turn it upside down so the base can dry out. When it has reached the leather-hard stage it is ready to turn into its final shape.

19

20

21

22

The walls are quite thick, but the excess clay will be turned away later.

The right-hand finger is used to smooth the rim.

A deep bowl has been formed to hold the water and oil.

The rim has a flat lip.

The rib removes excess clay from the wheel head and creates a bevel under the base.

Dampen the wheel head with a sponge. Using the rings cut into the aluminum wheel, center the lid upside down on the wheel. To check that the lid is central, hold your little finger against the rim and rotate the wheel. You should not feel any gaps. Using a ribbon tool, begin to form the bowl. Hold the tool in the right hand and rest the left hand on the lid with the left thumb against the tool to hold it steady. The wheel should be traveling fairly swiftly so less pressure is required to remove the clay.

Remove the edges of the base with the ribbon tool to form a smooth, curved, domed surface. Remove only small amounts of clay at a time.

Use the ribbon tool to remove the excess clay that was supporting the lip during throwing. The finished lid will look like a little hat with a brim. To remove the lid from the wheel, push it away from you. If it is still stuck down, rotate the wheel and place a thin-bladed knife under the rim. This will cut the clay a little and help to ease the lid off. Tidy up any finger marks with a sponge.

Take the basic mug shape when it is leather hard, and use something round to mark a curve on the wall of the pot, quite close to the base. Starting at the base, either push a mark onto the pot or draw around it.

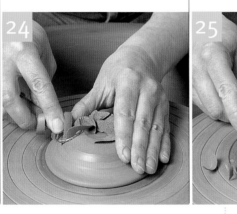

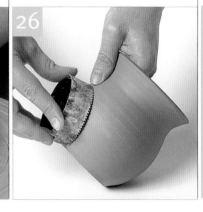

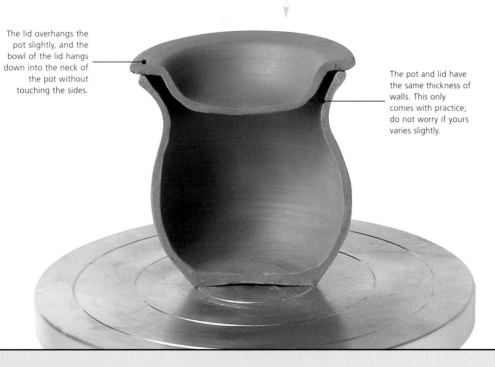

The lid overhangs the pot slightly, and the bowl of the lid hangs down into the neck of the pot without touching the sides.

The pot and lid have the same thickness of walls. This only comes with practice; do not worry if yours varies slightly.

Using this line as a guide, cut a circle of clay out with a craft knife. Cut a straight line across the base of the shape, just above the base of the mug form.

This cutout shape is the hole to insert the candle through. Use a hole cutter to make three decorative holes above the large shape.

Using hole cutters of various sizes, create a pattern on the opposite wall to the large cutout. This pattern is symmetrical, but any design can be used. Stars and moons are another good pattern, because when the candle is lit the light will shine through the holes.

Sponge the surface design lightly to remove any bits of loose clay from the design. Also sponge the inside to remove any debris from the decorating process.

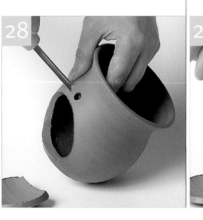
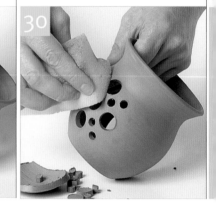

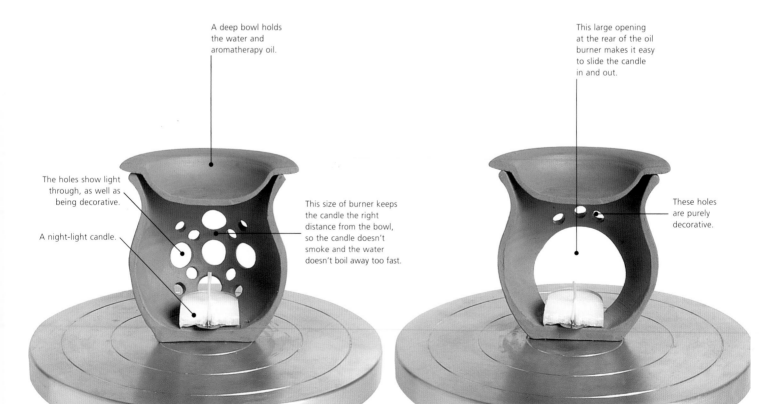

A deep bowl holds the water and aromatherapy oil.

This large opening at the rear of the oil burner makes it easy to slide the candle in and out.

The holes show light through, as well as being decorative.

A night-light candle.

This size of burner keeps the candle the right distance from the bowl, so the candle doesn't smoke and the water doesn't boil away too fast.

These holes are purely decorative.

Note

To use the oil burner, fill the lid with water and add three drops of your chosen aromatherapy oil. Place the burner on a non-flammable surface, light a night-light candle, and place it in the burner under the lid. The water will warm and scent the room. Add to the water later if required. Never leave a burning candle unattended or within the reach of children or pets.

This project shows how one simple form can create a range of finished objects. It is possible to create many different shapes other than these that would do the same job. Once you have mastered these few basic skills, use your imagination to create objects that are individual to you. You can never have too many different mugs and jugs when friends come to visit, so feel free to experiment.

A deep bowl has many uses, and matching individual bowls can be made using smaller balls of clay.

Deep Bowl

The almost straight sides of this bowl give a contemporary feel. The shape of the foot and a straight wall could be achieved by turning if any excess clay remains after throwing. Note the smooth inside curves.

An "S"-shaped wall is very elegant, though a little tricky to make. The inside and outside curves need to be in the same place to keep the walls an even thickness. It is possible to turn the outside wall, but when the pot is upside down it could be difficult to know the exact shape inside.

A wide, sweeping curve is a very simple bowl form; the inside of this pot should have a perfect curve with no apparent line where the sides start to form. A curved throwing rib could be used on the inside of the bowl to achieve the perfect curve.

This shape would make an excellent soup bowl because the deep, enclosed shape would retain heat. It could also benefit from the addition of handles to aid in lifting when hot.

This bowl is finished on the wheel with no need for any turning later. The foot ring is shaped and finished on the wheel.

The unusual squared-off shape—with its bowl-like inner curve and steep walls—can initially disguise any unevenness in the roundness of the bowl, but ultimately a perfectly round bowl makes a better altered form. Alternatively, if a good round form is created in the first place, you may want to leave it as it is.

This bowl is made using 4 lbs (1.8kg) of clay, which should make a bowl approximately 6 inches (15cm) high and 10 inches (25cm) wide when still wet.

A rounded rim profile means there are no sharp edges where glaze may be chipped off.

The walls taper slightly toward the rim. Ideally, even thickness could be achieved through turning, but as we are altering the form it will not be possible or necessary.

A slightly wider wall at the base gives more support to the upper walls.

The heavy base gives stability to this deep vessel.

KEY

Pulling, lifting, and shaping movements

Pushing, thickening, and supporting movements

Once you have centered the clay (see pages 20–21), with the wheel turning swiftly press your right thumb into the center of the clay. Remember to leave a fairly thick base. As you push the clay outward to widen the pot, raise the thumb up a little to create a curved inner floor to the bowl, supporting the clay with your left hand. Run your fingers over the base of the pot to consolidate the clay at the base to prevent cracks when drying and firing.

Place the thumb of your left hand at the base of the pot on the outside and the fingers of the same hand inside it. Position your right hand on the rim of the pot and over the left hand to provide support. Squeeze the thumb and fingers of your left hand together slightly. Holding this position, slowly bring your left hand up the side of the pot, squeezing as you continue upward. The wheel should be rotating faster than the hands are moving upward. Rest the heel of the right hand on the rim of the bowl to help consolidate the clay.

This first lift should be almost vertical. The clay naturally wants to flare out into a bowl shape, but do not let this happen too soon in the forming process or the clay will become difficult to control. It is helpful to leave the clay at the rim slightly thicker so that when you widen the bowl there is plenty of clay to work with.

1

2

3

The right hand is helping to hold the left hand steady.

The left-hand fingers are on the inside of the pot and the thumb is at the base on the outside. They are squeezing together firmly, but carefully, to thin the clay.

The heel of the right hand rests on the pot, helping to shape and control it while the rest of the hand supports the left hand.

The curved base on the inside of the pot is more desirable than a flat bottom since you do not want corners to clean into, and it is also more pleasing to the eye.

The walls are starting to thin evenly, though there is still plenty of weight left for the lifting process.

There is still a lot of clay at the base of this pot to form the foot ring later.

Support the wall and rim of the pot from the inside with the left hand. With the fingers of the right hand, push a groove into the clay wall at the base of the bowl next to the wheel. Make sure the clay is well lubricated and keep your arms held tight to your body with your forearms resting on the edge of the wheel tray.

Squeeze together the thumb and fingers of your left hand immediately above the groove. Place the knuckle of the right hand under the bulge you have created, while the left fingers sit inside the bowl, inside the bulge and just above the knuckle of the right hand. Begin to force the bulge upward with the right knuckle pressing against the fingers of the left hand. The bulge travels up the bowl thinning the clay as it goes. Let your bowl begin to widen a little; the centrifugal force of the spinning wheel will do it for you. It is more a case of not forcing the clay inward, rather than forcing it outward.

Take the bulge of clay all the way to the rim of the pot. Gently squeeze and smooth the rim to consolidate and strengthen the clay. This prevents it from starting to split and "feather" in the final shaping.

4

5

6

The walls of the pot are still very thick, ready for the lifting process.

The left-hand fingers support the clay wall and the thumb holds the clay vertical.

The knuckle of the right hand is placed in the groove, ready to start lifting the clay bulge from the base upward.

The bulge of clay is forced out by the fingers and lifted upward by the knuckle.

The bowl is starting to widen and fill out.

The curved inner base to the pot is clearly visible. Be careful not to flatten this too much as the lifting process continues.

Repeat the lifting process. Each time you start with the bulge at the base and push in with your fingers you are decreasing the width of the base, making it narrower. With practice, quite narrow bases can be achieved. Remember to keep the clay lubricated, and sponge out any excess water gathered inside.

Gradually the bowl gets taller and wider. Do not try to make this happen quickly; it is a slow, gentle process. Any sudden or quick movements are likely to send the bowl off balance and result in losing the pot, as it is almost impossible to collar a large wide form, such as this, back in. Reduce the speed of the wheel as the bowl gets wider. This, in turn, means the hands must also work slower. After two lifts the pot should be slightly taller than the finished bowl will be, as some height will be lost during the widening and shaping.

Before you begin to swell the body of the bowl, form the foot ring. First remove any excess clay from the wheel head with a throwing rib. Next, create a bevel under the base of the pot using the point of the rib at an angle to remove a sliver of clay. Then, press a curved corner of the rib into the clay above the bevel. This creates a ridge of clay at the base of the pot. If it has a sharp edge it can be smoothed with the fingers.

A little more weight is left at the rim to provide enough clay to widen the form later.

The knuckle is in position, ready for another lift.

The walls are straight at this point, ready for another lift to thin them further.

Using the throwing rib, you can now start to form the final shape of the bowl walls. Starting above the newly formed foot ring, use the rib on the outside of the bowl and the fingers of the left hand on the inside. Push the clay against the rib to smooth and shape. The rib and fingers need to travel up the clay wall together, all the way to the rim. The rim at this stage should be slightly flared out to its final width. You may need to do this a couple of times to get the desired shape.

In the final shaping the fingers of the left hand force the clay against the rib in the right hand. The rib is just supporting the clay and forming a smooth curve on the outside. With the wheel traveling fairly slowly, carefully swell the bowl out until it is as wide as the rim and the flare in the rim disappears. Do not rush this final finishing. Sponge out any water from inside, and the throwing is now finished. The bowl could be cut from the wheel now if you do not want to make the final square bowl.

Using the sharp corner of the throwing rib it is possible to create an interesting spiral on the surface of the bowl. Slowly rotate the wheel and hold the point of the rib on the surface of the bowl above the foot ring. Draw the rib upward creating a spiral groove in the bowl. Be careful not to push too hard, as only a light touch is needed to mark the surface of a wet pot. The slower you do this the more grooves you will get.

To achieve a more unusual square appearance, use the first finger of the right hand to press a vertical groove into the inner surface of the bowl starting at the bottom and moving quickly upward. Repeat the process on the opposite side of the bowl. Halfway between the two grooves create another, and repeat on the final side, dividing the bowl into four sections. This effect can be enhanced later. When the bowl has dried a bit, the walls could be tapped flatter with the hands or a flat piece of wood.

The bowl now has a smooth and sweeping uninterrupted inner curve.

The foot ring has been formed using the rib. This cross section shows the profile of the foot ring, sometimes called a roll foot. If you do not get this shape immediately, use the rib to scrape away more clay until you are happy with the result.

The fingers push the clay against the rib and slowly swell the bowl form outward.

The finished bowl will be easier to remove from the wheel if it can glide on a film of water. Flood the wheel head and wire the bowl off. Keep the wire taut and completely flat with the wheel head as you pull it toward you. With dry hands around the base, slide the bowl across the wheel and lift it onto a dry board. If you have distorted the shape, just give a gentle squeeze on the opposite sides to straighten it up. If it is very floppy, leave it on the wheel for an hour or throw the bowl on a bat (see page 35).

During drying, once the rim of the bowl has hardened, it would be beneficial to turn the bowl upside down so that it dries more evenly. To smooth the base, run your fingers around it to remove any excess clay, or use a sponge. Do not oversponge the base, as this brings grit in the clay to the surface and makes it rough.

The spinning potter's wheel naturally encourages the clay to splay outward and form the basic shape of a shallow bowl.

Shallow Bowl

A straight-sided open cone shape is easy to hold, so no handles are necessary. The depth of the foot ring on this bowl lifts the form up off the table, enabling us to see under it. The deep foot ring could be added later as the base would have to be left very thick to create enough depth from which to form it.

If a shallow bowl has a wide base it could be a soup plate, but it might need an extra foot ring to support the center to stop the base from sagging during firing. Simple forms like this are often the most elegant.

This low bowl can also be used as a saucer with the simple forming of a slight hollow for a teacup to sit in. This can be done at the throwing stage using a throwing rib, or formed at the same time that the base is turned.

The final shaping of the wall of the bowl is when the final profile of the bowl is determined. It could be left more vertical, creating a deeper bowl, or pulled wider and lower to make something approaching a plate. A rounded foot ring gives an interesting twist to this bowl profile.

A smooth, flowing inner curve is essential to a perfect shallow bowl form.

This shallow bowl is about as low as a bowl can go without becoming a plate, but obviously you can change the angle of the walls to create many different bowls. The inside of the form in this case is more important than the outside because it is the first thing you see. Ideally, the curve on the inside should not show strong changes in direction; it should flow smoothly from rim to rim. The outside of the bowl can be turned away later.

This bowl is made using 2 lb (900g) of clay, which should make a bowl that is approximately 2½ inches (6.5cm) high and 9 inches (23cm) wide when freshly made and still wet.

The extra weight that was supporting the clay during throwing has been turned away and formed into a foot ring.

The base has been turned away leaving just a foot ring touching the table. The base and walls are of even thickness.

KEY

⬅ Pulling, lifting, and shaping movements

⬅ Pushing, thickening, and supporting movements

First, center the clay (see pages 20–21). Using the side of the right hand, push down on the clay to create a depression in the center, then start to move the hand outward, pushing the clay away from the center. Tuck the left arm into the body and keep the forearm on the rim of the wheel tray. This locks the arm so the hand can steady the clay wall that is being pushed across the wheel and give support to the right hand to prevent any wobble. Keep the right elbow high in the air to give a downward pressure. Leave the base fairly thick, as it will be turned away later.

Once a wall of clay has been created, use the fingers of the right hand to push the clay at the base of the bowl down firmly against the wheel to further consolidate the base.

Now the walls of the bowl need to be created. Place the fingers of the left hand on the inside of the pot and the thumb on the outside, and the right hand over the left to support it. Gently squeeze the clay together between the thumb and fingers of the left hand. Remember to lubricate the clay with water, especially under the wall of clay, as it can soon dry and begin to snag on the thumb.

1

2

3

The right hand exerts a downward pressure, consolidating the base of the pot.

A wall of clay is formed as the right hand moves outward.

The left hand provides support for the clay and for the right hand.

A thick wall of clay has been formed from which to shape the bowl wall later.

The fingers push down on the base to consolidate the clay and to prevent cracking later.

Leave the base of this bowl thick, as you will turn it away later.

Resting both arms on the rim of the wheel tray, continue to squeeze the thumb and fingers of the left hand together, then let the hand travel up the wall of the pot in an upward and outward direction. As your hands travel upward, the clay bulge that has formed will decrease in size, so less pressure is required to thin the clay. Do not over-squeeze at the base of the wall, as some clay needs to be left to support the low wall.

Two lifts should be sufficient to thin the walls of this bowl. With practice it is possible to thin the walls to the correct size with just one lift on a ball of clay this size. Take care that the fingers inside do not create any indents in the walls or base to form a perfect internal curve. Remember to lubricate the hands and bowl at all times.

The walls of the bowl are steeper at this stage than in the finished item. Gently press down on the inside wall of the bowl with the left fingers against the right fingers on the outside. Alternatively, you could use a curved rib to form the inside surface.

Hold the flat edge of a throwing rib on the spinning wheel and push a pointed corner of the rib lightly under the base of the pot to create a bevel and remove excess clay from the wheel head. It is easier to do this now before the wall is lowered further, as it may be difficult to get a tool under the bowl wall when the shaping is finished.

The right hand is pressing on the rim of the bowl consolidating the clay and supporting the left hand.

A bulge of clay is being squeezed and thinned as the hands travel up the clay.

The base is left thick to be turned later.

Support the outside wall of the bowl with the rib as the fingers push down on the inside to lower the wall to its final height. This movement should start from the base of the pot and work up toward the rim very slowly. The wheel should be rotating slowly at this stage. The inside curve of this bowl is the most important because the outside can be turned into the right profile later, so don't worry if you have left too much clay at the wall base. Gently smooth the rim of the bowl with your fingers to finish.

The bowl is now finished, but while it is still on the wheel, make two lines on the inside surface with a knife. Only a light mark is needed. Revolve the wheel quite slowly at this stage so as not to force the bowl to widen any further. The marks should be about 1 inch (2.5cm) apart.

Flood the wheel head with water and wire the bowl off, keeping the wire taut and completely flat as you pull it toward you. This will drag water under the bowl making it easier to slide the pot off the wheel. Dry your hands and gently push the bowl across the wheel with the left hand onto the right hand, and place it on a dry bat. If it does not move easily, wire it again and try once more. This method of removal takes a little practice, so you may want to throw your bowls on wooden bats (see page 35).

Let the bowl dry until the rim is stiff. Turn it over and let it dry a little more. Once the clay is stiff but still damp it can be turned. Dampen the wheel and the rim of the pot and center it upside down on the wheel. To check that the bowl is central, hold your little finger against the rim of the bowl and rotate the wheel. It will be obvious if the size of the gap between the finger and the bowl varies as the bowl rotates. The damp wheel and the air trapped under the bowl help to hold it on by suction.

8

9

10

11

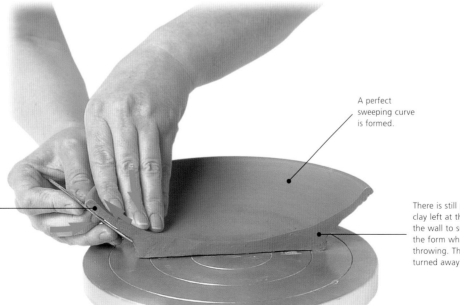

A perfect sweeping curve is formed.

The clay wall profile is formed using the rib for support as the fingers shape the final inside curve.

There is still plenty of clay left at the base of the wall to support the form while throwing. This will be turned away later.

Use a ribbon tool to turn the base. The wheel should be rotating very swiftly while turning is in progress. This can seem quite frightening initially, so start a bit slower but try to increase the speed: it will make turning much easier. Holding the ribbon tool in the right hand, first remove any stray bits of clay from around the edges of the base. Rest the left fingers on the bowl for stability and the thumb on the tool to lock it in position. Hold the arms tightly into the body to keep them steady.

Use the ribbon tool to trim away excess clay at the base of the wall, thus narrowing the base and giving the foot ring a definite shape. Take the base in as narrow as you require. This measurement is difficult to gauge, since every bowl is different, but will come with practice. This bowl is very low and the underneath will not be visible most of the time, so do not worry about it too much.

To ensure the profile of the outside curve matches the inside, use the ribbon tool to turn the clay away from the walls of the pot. If you find it difficult to visualize the inside of the form, turn some clay away then remove the bowl from the wheel, check the inside and feel the thickness with your fingers. This will tell you how much clay to remove. Recenter the bowl on the wheel to restart turning. This all takes a little time and practice, but you will soon become confident about how much clay to remove.

The next step is to hollow out the base. Using the ribbon tool again, start at the middle and work outward gently removing clay. Leave a band of about ⅜ inch (1cm) wide for the foot ring. It is best to remove clay a little at a time. Be careful not to remove too much or press down too hard as you may go through the base of the pot. The hollowed base of the pot should also follow the curve of the inside of the bowl, so it should dip down toward the foot ring on the inside.

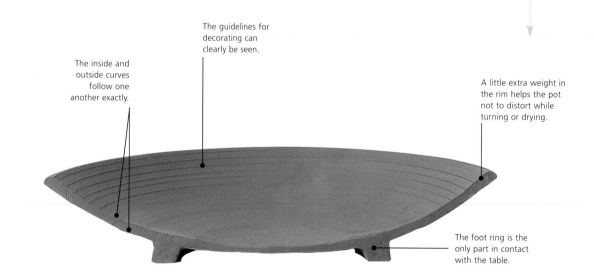

The inside and outside curves follow one another exactly.

The guidelines for decorating can clearly be seen.

A little extra weight in the rim helps the pot not to distort while turning or drying.

The foot ring is the only part in contact with the table.

To ensure the bowl sits flat when it is finished, check the foot ring is level using a flat ribbon tool to remove any bumps or bits of turning that have stuck there. Smooth any sharp corners that have formed on the foot ring.

Use a sharp craft knife to cut the final decoration between the two guidelines marked earlier. Support the clay wall with the left hand so the pressure of the knife does not distort the rim. Be careful not to cut your fingers that are underneath and out of sight. If you find the clay is too hard use a plant mister to spray the walls with water. Let this soak in and try again. This pattern is a collection of triangles and rectangles, because straight lines are easier to cut than curves.

This shallow bowl is probably most useful as a decorative piece, since small contents held by it could fall through the holes. It could be used as a candle dish or hung on the wall. Deeper or more elaborate foot rings could be added to create many different profiles. Alternatively, without the pierced work, handles or lugs could be added to the rim to transform it into a serving platter.

Candlesticks are no longer necessary items in everyday life, but they still make worthy decorative objects.

Candlestick

This candlestick has a wide, raised dish to collect any dripping wax. It could be thrown in one go, similar to making a lid, or the base could be made separately and added later. The possibilities for making and adding your own style to this shape are endless.

Very large versions of this traditional ribbed form are used to hold church candles. The base needs to be hollow because a solid form this large may explode during firing. When throwing, the thumb goes right to the bottom in the opening stage so a cone is formed that could then be sealed at the top to form the bowl.

The main form of this elaborate candelabra would be thrown separately to the side. Handles can be used to make loops to support other thrown candleholders. More holders could be added as long as the object as a whole was stable, otherwise it could present a fire risk.

This candleholder is basically a simple saucer with a depression in the center in which to stand a candle. This is a good holder for wide-based or unusual shaped candles.

Candlesticks can be found in a multitude of shapes and sizes. The candlestick in this project is known as a "Wee Willie Winkie," after the nursery rhyme. It is very functional, with a large handle that is easy to grip—it was traditionally used to illuminate the staircase as you went up to bed—and a wide drip tray to collect falling wax.

When making candlesticks, remember that the size and shape of the candles you are going to use should be taken into consideration.

This candlestick is made using 1lb (450g) of clay, which should make a candlestick approximately 2 inches (5cm) high and 6½ inches (16cm) wide when still wet.

The raised candleholder is wide enough to hold a standard candle in place.

A wide loop handle to place the fingers under makes for easy carrying and keeps the fingers well away from hot dripping wax.

A wide, flat base makes the candlestick stable and helps prevent accidents, although a burning candle should never be left unattended.

KEY

← Pulling, lifting, and shaping movements

← Pushing, thickening, and supporting movements

Centre the clay (see pages 20–23). Press the side of the right hand down into the clay, slightly away from the centre, supporting the outside with the left hand. This leaves a hill of clay in the middle and forms walls on the outside. The wheel should be moving fairly swiftly at this stage, and remember to lubricate the clay with water.

Continue using the side of the right hand and fingers to press the clay wall outwards, creating a flat, level base, but leaving a knob of clay in the centre to form the candleholder. The left hand still provides support to the clay wall as it moves outwards.

Squeeze the clay wall with the left-hand fingers on the inside and thumb on the outside to consolidate and strengthen it. Use the right hand on top of the left to provide support. Use the fingers of the left hand to push down on the base of the candlestick to compress the clay there also. Leave the wall thick to be shaped later.

Press the first finger of the right hand into the centre of the rotating clay to start to form the candleholder. Widen the hole slightly while supporting it with the fingers of the left hand. Make this clay knob into a small vase form.

The right hand pushes down away from the centre of the revolving clay mass.

A knob of clay is left in the middle, to form the holder later.

A wall of clay is being formed.

The first finger of the right hand pushes into the centre of the knob.

The base has been thinned to its final thickness.

The wall is left thick and heavy to form a rim later.

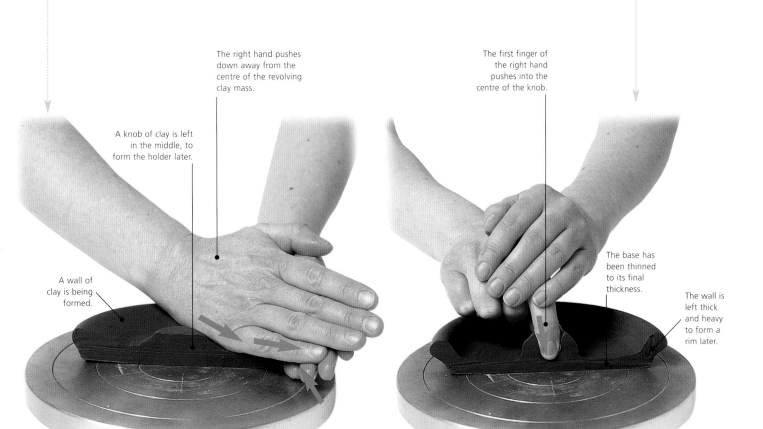

Use the index finger of the left hand to push a small bulge out in the wall of the central pot form above the base. Place the little finger of the right hand under the bulge and push it upward. It is such a small pot that to try and use the knuckle would be difficult. The clay is thinned as the height increases. Try not to use too much water for lubrication because it is difficult to get it out of such a small pot with a sponge.

Use the fingers to shape the holder and form a rim. This should be done slowly, though the wheel should be moving fairly swiftly, as it is small and in the center of the wheel. If the candleholder has a neck formed into it, as in this example, it is more likely to grip the candle placed there.

To form the outside rim of the candlestick, place the thumb of the left hand under the lip of the rim and the left fingers on the inside with the right hand on top of the left. Squeeze the clay between the left thumb and fingers and draw the clay rim outward and slightly upward. This rim creates a place to attach a handle on the holder, as well as being decorative.

Create a bevel under the base of the pot using the throwing rib at an angle to remove a sliver of clay, making it easier to wire it off the wheel. Flood the wheel head with water, keep the wire taut and pull it toward you. If you do this a couple of times, a thin layer of water will cause the pot to aquaplane so it can be pushed across the wheel with the left hand onto the right. If you are not confident about moving a wider pot from the wheel, this candlestick could be made on a wooden bat (see page 35).

The right hand finger pushes the bulge upward.

A small pot is being made to hold the candle.

The left-hand thumb is under the rim and the fingers are inside the form. Squeezing them together thins the clay and forms the rim.

The index finger of the left hand pushes out a bulge in the pot wall.

The right hand helps to steady the left.

The walls are thick to form a rim later.

The candleholder is now finished.

When the candlestick has dried to leather hard, a handle can be added. An extruded section is used here, but see pages 148–153 for other options. Use a craft knife to crosshatch the area on the neck where you want to attach the handle. Dab some slurry onto the crosshatched area, attach one end of the handle and smooth the join. Form a loop and attach the other end to the rim of the candlestick and smooth as before. The loop should be large enough that you can safely hold the candlestick when the candle is lit.

9

This candlestick does not require any turning. A shape like this would be difficult to turn as the candleholder extends above the rim of the plate. The outer rim of the candlestick is quite thin and needs no excess clay left under it for support during throwing. If any excess clay is left try to remove it with a rib before removing it from the wheel. This is just one example of a candlestick, many other designs could be tried, the only feature necessary is a holder for the candle that will keep it safely in position.

Plates are an important part of any thrower's repertoire. Their domestic use should be considered when creating the form.

Plate

This is a strong shape. The rim does not overhang the base too much, so the plate is unlikely to collapse during making or firing. Since the base is quite wide and the plate has a turned foot ring, another inner foot ring has been turned to add extra support so the plate base does not sag.

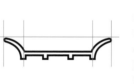

This small rim is not very decorative, but is easy to make. Such rims are usually found on large serving platters or pizza plates. The inside base should be flat, whereas underneath it should be slightly hollow. Only the outside edge makes contact with the table.

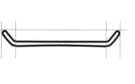

This sweeping curved rim is very elegant, but reasonably difficult to make. It requires extra clay at the base of the wall to support it during throwing. That then needs to be turned away. This plate is quite deep, so it could be used as a soup plate.

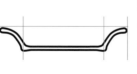

A narrow rim is made into a feature by the groove in its surface. A little extra clay needs to be left under the rim during throwing to support this shape. Another groove can be formed as a foot ring when turning.

The hand movements used to make a plate are very different from that of taller forms. It would follow that plates should be easier to make, but to make a flat plate with an even base takes practice. The plate, however, gives an excellent surface on which to decorate. Historically, plates were, and are, used to commemorate important events.

Handmade plates are always heavier than their industrial equivalent, but this shouldn't be seen as something negative. Attempts to make very thin and light plates often fail because "flatware" is prone to twisting and warping. One advantage of a heavier plate is that it keeps food hotter for longer.

This plate is made using 3 lb 8 oz (1.6kg) of clay, which should make a plate that is approximately 11½ inches (29cm) wide when freshly made and still wet.

The plate needs to be of an even thickness. If the rim is too thick, its weight may cause it to slump during firing.

The outer edge of the foot ring is the only part that actually touches the table.

The base of the plate is slightly hollowed so that it doesn't make contact with the table, making the plate less likely to wobble or rock.

KEY

← Pulling, lifting, and shaping movements
← Pushing, thickening, and supporting movements

Plates are usually made on wooden bats because it is nearly impossible to remove them from the wheel head immediately after making without distorting them. Secure a wooden bat to the wheel head (see page 35) and center the clay (see pages 20–21). The wheel should be moving swiftly during plate making, as there are no vertical walls to be thrown off balance. Press down with the heel of the right hand, creating a depression in the center of the clay. Support the clay wall on the outside with the left hand, without exerting any pressure. Then push the clay outward across the bat. Keep the right elbow high to help apply downward pressure.

Continue to push the clay outward using the side of the right hand. A small hill of clay is left in the center of the plate, but this will be incorporated into the base later. It is easier to remove a lump than it is to replace clay in the center if you go too deep when forming the base.

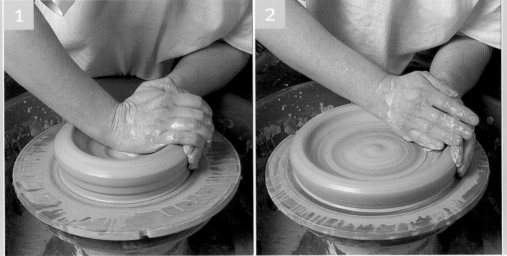

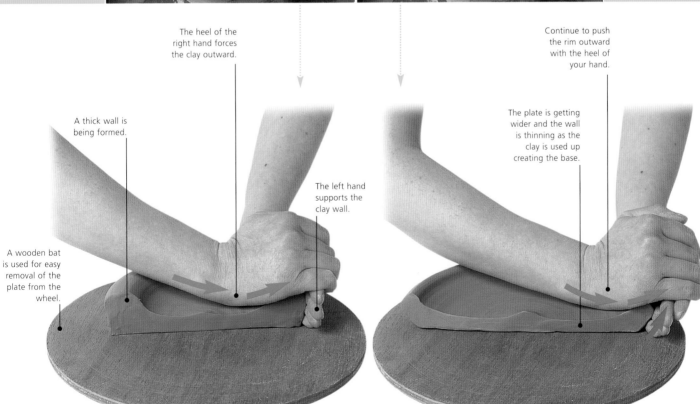

The heel of the right hand forces the clay outward.

A thick wall is being formed.

The left hand supports the clay wall.

A wooden bat is used for easy removal of the plate from the wheel.

Continue to push the rim outward with the heel of your hand.

The plate is getting wider and the wall is thinning as the clay is used up creating the base.

Use the side of the right hand to press the hill in the center into the base of the plate by squashing it down and moving it slowly outward. Continue moving the hands outward, away from the center, making the base as flat as possible. Lubricate the plate regularly, as such a wide surface soon uses up water and begins to snag on the fingers. You may find the water is flung over the edge as the plate widens. This is rather messy but unavoidable.

With the right hand on top of the left, exert downward pressure on the fingers to consolidate the base of the plate and further flatten it. It is very important when making plates to compress the base well, as a wide expanse of flat clay such as this is put under great stress during drying and firing and might crack. The most common crack is an "S" shape and is a result of the clay not being properly consolidated during throwing. Keep running your fingers slowly over the base until any lumps or hollows disappear.

Place the thumb of the left hand on the outside of the ridge at the top of the plate and the fingers on the inside. Rest the right hand on the ridge and over the left. Gently squeeze the thumb and fingers of the left hand together to begin to form the rim, while the right gently presses down to consolidate the clay. The inner profile of the plate should also be formed at this stage. This plate has a fairly definite change in direction, from a horizontal base to a vertical wall.

Before the rim is finished, use a throwing rib to smooth the base for the last time and remove any remaining lumps. Starting from the middle, move the rib slowly outward across the base of the plate using gentle pressure so that you don't form grooves in the surface. This action also helps compress the clay further and moves any water or slurry outward so it can easily be sponged off.

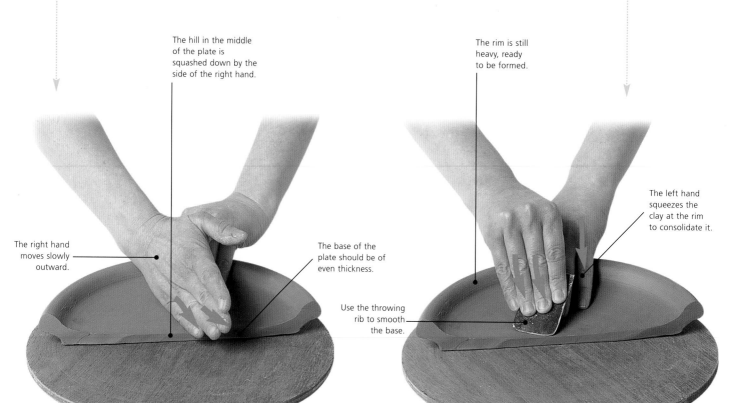

The hill in the middle of the plate is squashed down by the side of the right hand.

The rim is still heavy, ready to be formed.

The right hand moves slowly outward.

The base of the plate should be of even thickness.

The left hand squeezes the clay at the rim to consolidate it.

Use the throwing rib to smooth the base.

Use the rib to create a slight bevel under the plate to guide the cutting wire by holding the flat edge of the rib on the spinning wheel and pushing it slightly under the base of the plate. It is best to do this now because once the rim of the plate is formed it will be difficult to get to. Take care when using the rib close to a wooden bat, as it may snag on the grain of the wood, causing the rib to jump up and damage the plate.

Position the fingers of the left hand on the inside and the thumb under the rim with the right hand over the left to steady it. Gently squeeze the rim between the left thumb and fingers and draw the clay outward and slightly upward, away from the base. Do this very gently and gradually. The wheel should be rotating more slowly, but not too slow. It is now a long way around the pot—one revolution takes longer than before—so when drawing the clay out, do it slowly. If your hands move too fast, the rim will become uneven.

Continue to shape the rim, making sure it is well lubricated, as any snagging will rip it away from the plate or cause it to go off center. You may find this whole process easier to perform using the right hand to squeeze and form the rim. Use whichever method is most comfortable for you.

The rim is bending upward at this point, so use the rib to lower it to its final shape. Support the clay with the left hand as you press down with the rib on top. Only light pressure is required so the rim doesn't flop. The throwing is now complete. Wire under the plate and pull it toward you. Remove the wooden bat from the wheel with the plate still on it. When the plate is dry enough that it will not be distorted, wire it again and transfer it to a dry board. Once the clay is stiff but still damp it can be turned.

The left hand grips the clay and gently squeezes it outward.

There is still weight in the rim waiting to be thinned.

The left hand supports the clay from underneath as the rim is flattened by the rib.

The rim is thinning, moving outward, and rising upward.

There is still excess clay under the rim to support the lip. This will be turned away later.

The plate also needs to be turned on a bat, as the wheel head is not wide enough to support the rim. Resecure the bat to the wheel head. Dampen the bat and the rim of the plate and center the plate upside down on the bat. Hold your little finger against the rim and rotate the wheel. The gap between the finger and the plate rim should remain constant. If not, reposition the plate, remembering to dampen the rim again. The damp clay traps air under the plate and holds it in position by suction.

Using a ribbon tool, gently scrape a thin layer of clay from the base. Hold the tool in the right hand and rest the left hand on the pot with the thumb against the tool to steady it. The wheel should be traveling fairly swiftly. Hold your arms tightly into your body and rest your forearms on the rim of the wheel tray to help hold the tool still as you slowly work from the center outward. Do not let the tool rise and fall with bumps on the plate, as these are what you are trying to remove.

Use a curved-edged ribbon tool held in and guided by both hands to remove the excess clay that was supporting the rim. The clay here is quite thick so do not worry about removing it and accidentally going through the plate. You are trying to form a nice curve from the foot to the rim. Remove the excess clay gradually, starting at the rim and working up to the foot each time, removing more clay where it is thickest or uneven.

To aid with glazing later, turn a roll foot onto the plate. Use the ribbon tool to slightly undercut the base and trim away some clay to create a slight overhang. Trim a little more until you are happy with the shape. Ideally, only the very outside edge of the base should touch the table, so the middle of the base needs to dip slightly. To achieve this, remove a little more clay with the ribbon tool, working outward from the center. Reduce the amount you remove as you work outward. Stop short of the edge.

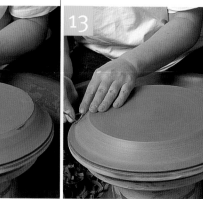

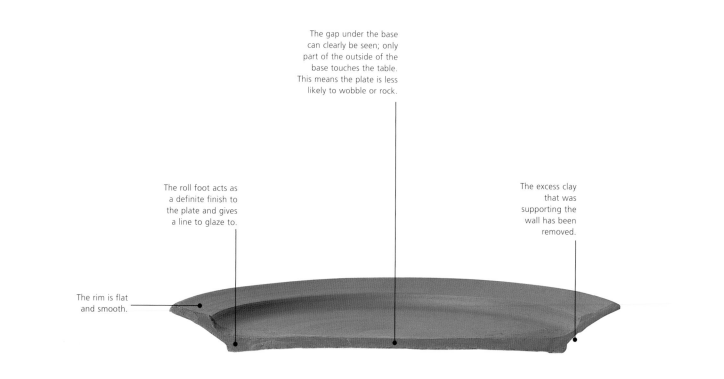

The gap under the base can clearly be seen; only part of the outside of the base touches the table. This means the plate is less likely to wobble or rock.

The roll foot acts as a definite finish to the plate and gives a line to glaze to.

The excess clay that was supporting the wall has been removed.

The rim is flat and smooth.

To test the dip, place a straight edge across the base. It should touch clay at either side but a gap should be seen in the middle. When turning, try not to press down on the base of the plate too heavily, as you may distort the shape and push the base in. Remove the plate from the bat and check the profile and the base. It is amazing how different it will appear when the right way up, and you may feel that you need to shape the underside a little more. Just recenter and continue until you are happy.

The plate, or charger, as wide-rimmed plates are known, provides an ideal canvas for decoration. In this example, a layer of liquid clay (called "slip") in a contrasting color has been poured over the inside of the leather-hard plate. When this has dried, it is scraped away to reveal the clay underneath. Any design can be cut in this way. It is similar to using scrapper board. This technique is called sgraffito.

The cheese bell is a decorative and functional means of storing and serving cheese. A smaller version can be used for butter.

Cheese Bell

This cheese bell is low and wide. It looks better with this type of strap handle on one side, rather than with a knob. A smaller plate and cover would make an excellent butter dish.

Some considerable skill is required to make this covered server because great accuracy is needed to make the two parts fit together. However, the tight fit makes it best for storage. The position of the join between the plate and the cover could be moved, so this could be a casserole or deep serving dish.

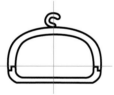

A deep bell like this could also be used as a covered serving dish for vegetables. A gallery is formed in the plate when thrown, giving the cover an elevated platform on which to sit.

This is a more complicated plate shape to make. The locating ridge must be formed out of the base as the plate is thrown. It also requires greater accuracy in measuring when making the cover. The tight fit, however, is particularly advantageous to keeping cheese fresh.

Making the cover provides an opportunity to create interesting knobs and handles as decorative additions, just so long as it can still be easily cleaned, as function is important to such a practical object. It is also a spacious area to decorate and can take quite large designs and patterns.

This cheese bell uses the plate made on pages 74–79, and a cover made from 3 lb (1.5kg) of clay, which should make a cover large enough to fit the plate.

A hollowed out decorative knob dries evenly. A thick solid knob would dry very slowly and could explode if placed in the kiln while still damp on the inside.

A heavy rim makes the cover strong and stops it getting chipped. It also gives a definite finish to the "bell."

The cover should fit neatly inside the rim of the plate.

A smooth, flat plate that it is practical to cut cheese on is required.

KEY

⬅ Pulling, lifting, and shaping movements

⬅ Pushing, thickening, and supporting movements

Take the plate made on pages 74–79, and use calipers to measure the inside base. Make sure the calipers are tight and won't move so the measurement is accurate. This will become the measurement for the width of the cover. Remove the bat from the wheel with the plate on it. Place a new wooden bat on the wheel head (see page 35). Throwing the cover on a bat means you are unlikely to distort the shape when removing it from the wheel, so it will still fit on the plate correctly.

Center the clay for the bell (see pages 20–21). Lubricate the clay with water and push the thumb of the right hand into the middle of the revolving clay. The depth of the base needs to be thicker rather than thinner, as we are going to turn the base later. Push the thumb outward to widen the hole, supporting the clay wall with the left hand.

Place the left thumb at the base of the pot on the outside, and the fingers on the inside. Place the right hand on top of the clay wall and the left hand to provide support. Squeeze the thumb and fingers of the left hand together with a firm but even pressure. Tuck your arms into your body for extra support.

Squeeze the clay upward between the left thumb and fingers. Remember to keep the vertical movement of the hands slower than the revolving wheel. The wheel should be spinning fairly quickly. As the clay walls increase in height the clay between your fingers and thumb will decrease, so less pressure is required to squeeze it. As you approach the top, leave a ridge of clay to form the heavy rim. Do not overthin the clay by squeezing too hard. Lubricate the clay as needed.

1

2

3

4

The right thumb pushes the clay outward, widening the hole.

This is essentially a bowl form, so a sweeping inner curve needs to be created.

The fingers of the left hand squeeze and lift the clay wall.

The base is left fairly thick for turning later.

The rim is left heavy to form the base of the cover later.

The left hand supports the clay wall.

Extra clay at the base will be turned away later.

Thin the walls further by using the knuckle of the right hand on the outside of the pot and the fingers of the left hand inside it. Press a bulge of clay out at the base of the bowl with the left fingers and place your right knuckle under the bulge. With even pressure and your arms tucked into your body to hold your hands steady, begin to push the bulge up the wall of the pot. Continue to push the left fingers outward as the knuckle pushes upward, thus thinning the clay and increasing the height of the walls.

Remember to leave enough clay at the rim to form the base of the cover. Squeeze this ridge of clay with the fingers and thumb of the left hand while squashing it downward with the side of the right hand to compress and con-solidate the clay to finish the rim and give it strength. Continue the lifting process until you have thinned the clay sufficiently. The bowl will be slightly taller at this point, as some height will be lost in the shaping process.

Using a throwing rib on the outside of the bowl wall and the fingers of the left hand on the inside, begin to swell the bowl out and smooth the walls by squeezing and pushing the clay outward onto the rib. Use the left thumb over the rim on the outside to support the wall. Be careful not to widen the rim too much as it may not fit on the plate later. It is easier to widen the bowl than try to make it narrower later.

5

6

7

The left fingers force the clay outward.

The rim is left as a definite ridge.

The right knuckle pushes the bulge upward.

The base remains thick, ready to be turned later.

The left thumb supports the wall of the bowl.

The walls are of even thickness, tapering only slightly toward the rim.

The left fingers push the clay against the rib.

The right hand holds the rib against the outside wall of the pot.

Use the sharp corner of the rib to define the rim by creating a groove in the wall just below it, pushing from the inside with the left fingers and supporting the rim with the left thumb. Flatten the rim on top slightly with the fingers to form a flat surface for the cover to sit on in the plate. Check the width of the bowl with the preset calipers. The width should be the same or slightly smaller to ensure a neat fit. If the bowl rim is not wide enough, gently ease it out until the correct diameter is achieved. Wire the cover, and remove the bat from the wheel with the cover still in place. Leave it to dry a little.

When the rim has dried sufficiently for it to be inverted without distortion, turn the cover upside down to dry. When the clay is leather hard—firm to the touch but still damp—dampen the rim and the wheel head so they stick together and cause suction, which will hold the cover firmly in place. Center the cover upside down on the bat. To check that the bowl is central, hold your little finger against the rim and rotate the wheel. It will be obvious if the size of the gap between the finger and the bowl varies as the bowl rotates. Stop the wheel and reposition the pot if necessary, remembering to dampen the rim.

Press a ribbon tool against the top of the cover to begin to form the outer curve. Hold the tool in the right hand and rest the left hand on the cover with the left thumb against the tool to hold it steady. The wheel should be moving quite quickly, as turning is easier and requires less pressure if there are more revolutions of the wheel. There is quite a lot of clay to remove, so do not worry as the ribbons of clay fly off into the tray.

8

9

10

The rib's sharp corner forms a definite shape to the rim.

The left-hand fingers support the clay and the thumb rests on the rib.

The rim is heavy but nicely rounded.

Continue turning with the ribbon tool until you achieve a smooth, bump-free, curved surface with even thickness to the walls. You can remove the cover and check the thickness, but you then have to recenter it before you can continue to turn. Until you are able to judge automatically, it is best to do this.

Once you are happy with the shape of the cover, you can throw the knob. Use a craft knife to crosshatch an area in the middle of the top of the cover. This creates a key to grip the clay that will form the knob. Roll a small ball of clay between the hands, dampen it slightly, and press it down onto the cross-hatched area. Using just a little water for lubrication, center the ball and shape it into a knob with the fingers (see pages 154–157). The wheel should be rotating fairly swiftly.

Continue shaping the knob. The knob in this project is solid and has a groove under it so it is easy to grip when in use. If the ball of clay drags on the fingers while shaping, use a little more water to lubricate. If you accidently tear the knob off, just start again. However, be careful not to overwet the newly turned cover because it will absorb water and quickly begin to soften, and may therefore distort.

Use a sponge to remove any excess water and slurry and to smooth the join between the knob and the cover. The cover is now finished. Carefully remove it from the wheel and leave to dry. Before it is completely dry, use a hole-making tool to hollow out the knob from the inside. This will help it to dry out evenly so it does not explode in the kiln, which a thick solid knob might do if it was still damp on the inside.

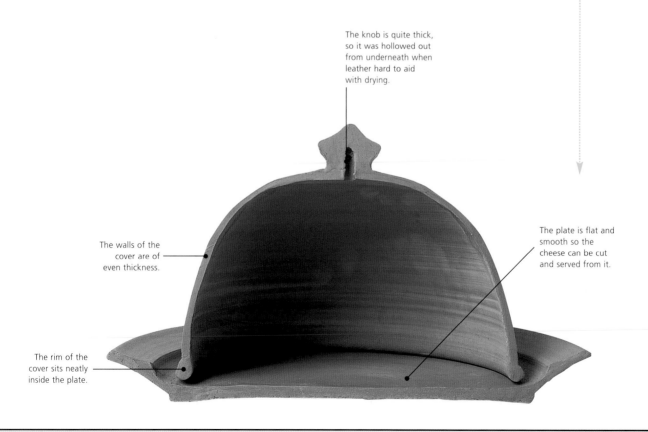

The knob is quite thick, so it was hollowed out from underneath when leather hard to aid with drying.

The walls of the cover are of even thickness.

The rim of the cover sits neatly inside the plate.

The plate is flat and smooth so the cheese can be cut and served from it.

Cheese is best served at room temperature, and a bell like this keeps it fresh in the short term. This is a simple dome and plate, but other plates and covers could be made to fit together to create all manner of interesting and varied combinations. A strap handle could replace the knob and the cover could be more conical than curved. As long as you measure the plate and cover so they fit together, you can invent your own cheese bell.

Important in the tradition of serving afternoon tea, the cake stand holds its treats above everything else on the table to make them the focal point.

Cake Stand

This deep bowl on a pedestal would make an excellent plant holder. Urns and jardinieres can be made in many shapes and sizes for outdoor and indoor use. Varying the size and shape of the bowl and pedestal can produce an infinite variety of forms. The only restricting factor is their stability, as they shouldn't be easily knocked over.

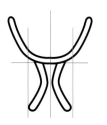

Placing a wide bowl on a pedestal can make a classical fruit bowl. It would look magnificent with grapes hanging down and fruit piled high in the center.

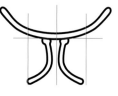

A small base topped with a bowl with handles would make an interesting serving dish. For hot food, a lid could be made to create a covered server.

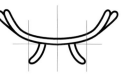

This smaller version of a bowl and pedestal is a wine goblet. Goblets can be formed from one piece of clay, but the base would have to be solid. Making a separate hollow base and cup and joining them together is a much more desirable alternative, especially if the goblet is quite large, as is this church communion goblet.

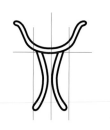

This cake stand is made in two sections, a plate and a pedestal, that are then joined together. When you start making joined forms the possibilities are endless, and this project illustrates the skills you need to go on to create a multitude of different forms. These techniques open up a variety of new shapes that would be impossible to create on the wheel in one go.

This cake stand uses the plate made on pages 74–77, before turning, and a pedestal made from 2 lb 8oz (1.2kg) of clay which should make a pedestal approximately 6 inches (2.5cm) high and 5 inches (2cm) wide when freshly made and still wet.

KEY

⬅ Pulling, lifting, and shaping movements

⬅ Pushing, thickening, and supporting movements

The rim on the plate helps to contain crumbs and is visually interesting.

A plate creates a flat and practical surface to serve a cake from.

A ridge in the pedestal highlights the change in direction of the curve in this tall base, as well as being decorative.

The wide base helps to give the cake stand stability while it is in use.

Throwing the pedestal on a wooden bat will prevent you from distorting this baseless form, which may happen if you try to remove it from the wheel while it is still wet. Secure a wooden bat to the wheel head (see page 35) and center the clay (see pages 20–21). Press the thumb of the right hand into the center of the revolving clay and push right down to the wooden bat: this pedestal is hollow, and formed upside down. Push the wall of clay outward to widen the hole, supporting the wall with the left hand on the outside. Remember to lubricate the hands with water regularly.

Place the thumb of the left hand at the base on the outside of the pot and the left fingers inside. Rest the right hand on the rim and over the left. Gently squeeze the left thumb and fingers together to thin the clay, and begin to steadily raise the left hand. Continue squeezing as you travel up the side of the pot. Push the clay inward with the right hand, resting it on the rim of the pot and consolidating the clay there. Leave a reasonably thick rim, as this will be the base of the pedestal.

The left hand supports the wall. This is very important when the pot has no base.

The thumb and fingers of the left hand squeeze the clay wall.

The right-hand thumb has pushed right down to the wheel head.

The walls are cone shaped, which makes the lifting process easier.

The pedestal is hollow and has no base.

The wall is thinning and increasing in height.

With the left-hand fingers still on the inside, push a bulge of clay outward at the base of the pot, next to the wooden bat. Place the knuckle of the right hand under the bulge on the outside and push it upward as the wheel rotates. Continue to push the bulge outward with the left hand as it rises into the path of the right knuckle. Use the right knuckle to also push the clay inward so it does not flare out. Continue to lubricate with water when necessary and mop out any excess water with a sponge.

Use the first finger of the right hand to smooth the rim of the pot, pushing lightly downward to flatten and consolidate the thick rim and give a smooth finish. Repeat the lifting process a couple of times to create a tall cylinder. Use a throwing rib to smooth the outer surface, remove excess water, and consolidate the clay wall. Support the clay on the inside with the fingers of the left hand and gently press against the rib on the outside.

Slow the wheel down to prevent the clay from widening further and to make it easier to control. Remember that all hand movements should also be slowed. Push the rib inward at the center of the pedestal to make it narrower. The pedestal should be trumpet shaped, the rim should be about 1 inch (2.5cm) wider than the base. The pedestal should also be about 1 inch (2.5cm) taller than the width of the rim. These are only rough measurements, so do not worry if your pedestal is slightly different.

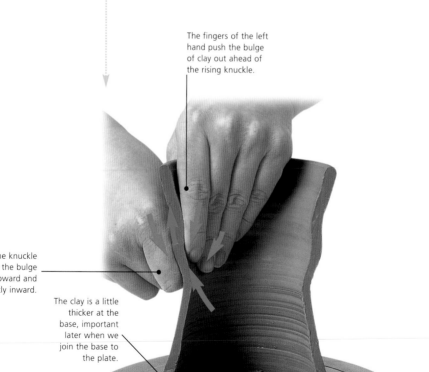

The fingers of the left hand push the bulge of clay out ahead of the rising knuckle.

The knuckle pushes the bulge upward and slightly inward.

The clay is a little thicker at the base, important later when we join the base to the plate.

Use the rib to form a decorative groove and ridge in the center of the pedestal. Push the clay out from the inside with the left fingers and carefully define using the rib on the outside. Do this very slowly so as not to distort the pot or knock it off center. Using the point of the rib at an angle, remove a sliver of clay to create a small bevel into the base to guide the cutting wire into later: this is not part of the finished pot as it has been in previous projects. Remove any excess water gathered in the pot.

The throwing of the pedestal is now finished. Remove the wooden bat from the wheel with the pedestal on it. Do not wire the pedestal off at this stage, as a pot with no base is easily distorted. Leave it for a couple of hours, or until the rim has stiffened. Then wire the pedestal; keep the wire taut and flat with the bat as you pull it toward you. Leave it on the bat until it is leather hard, stiff but still damp, when you can join it to the plate.

Take the plate made on pages 74–77, before it has been turned, and prepare it for turning in the same way (step 11, page 78). The base of this plate needs to be smooth and does not need a foot ring. Remove all the excess clay that was supporting the rim during throwing using a ribbon tool. Hold the tool in the right hand and rest the left hand on the plate and against the tool to hold it steady. The wheel should be moving fairly swiftly.

Continue to remove excess weight of clay, but keep the wall of even thickness. You want to achieve smooth, rounded curves that follow the internal shape of the plate. Remove the plate from the wheel and check the thickness of the walls. Before you recenter the plate on the wooden bat, it is advisable to place a pad of clay in the center of the bat as deep as the plate. This supports the center of the plate from underneath as you attach the pedestal. Otherwise, the weight and pressure you apply may push the base in a bit.

The left fingers push out while the rib defines the newly formed decorative ridge.

The left thumb can support the rim during shaping.

The rim has been left reasonably heavy to form the base when the cake stand is finished and placed the right way up.

Recenter the plate and with the wheel rotating slowly. Use a craft knife to lightly mark the base with concentric circles to help you place the pedestal in the center of the plate. The pedestal and base should be at the same stage of dryness so when they are joined they will continue to dry and shrink at the same rate and not crack apart. Remove the pedestal from its bat. The part of the pedestal that was attached to the wooden bat will now be attached to the plate, so do not worry if it is a bit untidy.

Find the guideline circle that is closest to the width of the pedestal and align the pedestal with it. Slowly spin the wheel to check it is centered in this position. Remove the pedestal. Crosshatch this area and the base of the pedestal with the craft knife to create a good key and give strength to the joining of the two parts.

Dab a layer of slurry from the wheel tray around the base of the pedestal. Use lots to make sure the two parts "glue" together well. Place the pedestal on the crosshatched area of the plate and firmly press it down into position. Be careful not to distort the shape of the plate base by pressing too hard.

Rotate the wheel slowly and press the first finger of the right hand onto the join to seal it. This also removes any excess slurry that may have squeezed out from the join. It is difficult when joining pieces together to get them both centered satisfactorily. Do not worry if you have a slight wobble, as this will not show when the pot is placed the right way up and finished. If, however, the wobble is very noticeable, you may want to remove the pedestal and recenter it before you seal the join.

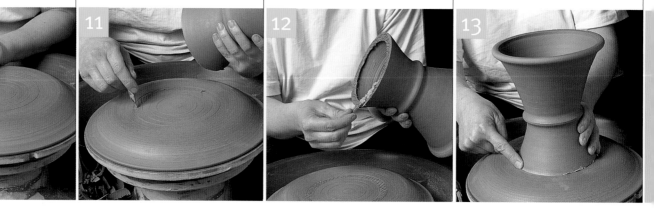

The extra thickness where the coil of clay was added to strengthen the join can be seen.

The plate has a smooth, flowing outer curve with no sharp edges.

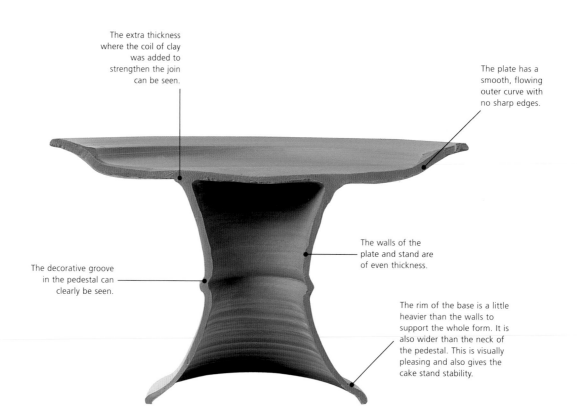

The decorative groove in the pedestal can clearly be seen.

The walls of the plate and stand are of even thickness.

The rim of the base is a little heavier than the walls to support the whole form. It is also wider than the neck of the pedestal. This is visually pleasing and also gives the cake stand stability.

Stop the wheel and roll out a thin coil of clay. Press this into the join, then rotate the wheel slowly and smooth the join with the first finger of the right hand. Lightly lubricate the finger and push the new clay well into the join, covering up any imperfections and giving a neat finish. To remove the finished cake stand from the wheel, gently push the plate part away from you. You may prefer to remove the bat with the cake stand on it and let it dry a little before turning it the right way up to prevent distorting it.

This is quite a tricky project. The two pots are themselves quite simple, but joining them creates difficulties. However, in the end, it is well worth it. As the pedestal is made upside down its proportions can be difficult to judge, but with practice this will become easier. This is quite a simple pedestal, but you could add as many decorative grooves or shapes as you like and change the height and width as you desire. Bowls could also be joined to pedestals in the same way to create fruit bowls. In fact, the possibilities are endless, as long as you remember the golden rule: two parts must always be of the same dryness when you join them.

A deep oval dish was traditionally used as a game pie dish. A thick crust of pastry was placed over the meat to seal in the moisture and flavor.

Oval Baking Dish

This complicated shape would be thrown as a baseless pot, shaped when drier, and placed on a rolled-out slab of clay. The base would be cut to shape and the pot stuck down. The biggest danger with this type of pot is making sure the base does not crack: because it has not been thrown it has not had the same forces and pressures applied to it as the walls.

To make a square shape, a four-pointed star of clay needs to be cut from the base and the sides pushed and flattened inward, until the base comes together. The joins need to be well sealed. The shape could be rectilinear, as well as square, and handles are an optional extra

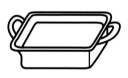

This shallow oval bowl is made in the same way as the dish in this project, but the walls have been pressed sharply inward along their longest side to create a new profile. The base profile remains oval.

Fruit pie dishes are traditionally quite flat and based on a plate design, but even these could be altered to make an oval plate as an alternative to the more traditional circle.

Many thrown shapes can be altered to form new shapes. This oval dish is thrown as a round dish and then has clay removed from the base to alter its shape. Alternatively, a wall with no base could be thrown and then attached to an irregular base rolled out separately.

If the dish is to be placed in an oven, then the choice of clay is very important (see pages 12–13). A simple shape is best for a functional piece that will need to be washed and cleaned easily.

This baking dish is made using 3 lb (1.5kg) of clay, which should make a dish that is approximately 4 inches (10cm) high and 8 inches (20cm) wide when freshly made and still wet.

The heavy rim prevents it from being easily chipped, and also acts as a rest for the pastry topping.

The deep shape allows for a lot of filling. The walls are of even thickness to ensure even heating.

The roll foot gives a definite finish to the dish and is an extra decorative feature on an otherwise plain pot.

KEY

Pulling, lifting, and shaping movements

Pushing, thickening, and supporting movements

This dish should be made on a wooden bat because it is difficult to remove from the wheel. Secure a wooden bat to the wheel head (see page 35) and center the clay (see pages 20–21). To open the ball of clay, push the heel of the right hand down into the center of the revolving clay. The wheel should be turning fairly quickly. Push the heel of the hand outward to form a wall. Support the outside wall as it forms with the left hand. Lubricate hands and clay well, as they can dry out easily during this stage of opening.

A thick wall of clay has now been formed. Use the fingers of the left hand to press down on the base of the pot to consolidate and strengthen the clay. This is particularly important because we are going to alter the base and it will be used in the oven, so it needs to be as strong as possible. Push the right-hand fingers down on the left hand to add extra pressure.

Place the thumb of the left hand at the base of the pot on the outside and the fingers on the inside. Place the right hand on top of the left to provide support. Squeeze the clay between the left fingers and thumb. Pull the left hand up the wall of the pot. Thin the clay as it rises and push inward to prevent the wide bowl flaring out too much. This heightens the wall of the pot. Leave a thick rim.

To increase the height of the walls and to thin the clay further, place the fingers of the left hand inside the pot and push out a small bulge at the base. Place the knuckle of the right hand under the bulge on the outside and push it upward as the wheel rotates. Make sure the vertical movement of the hands is slower than the rotation of the wheel, and lubricate the clay as needed.

1

2

3

4

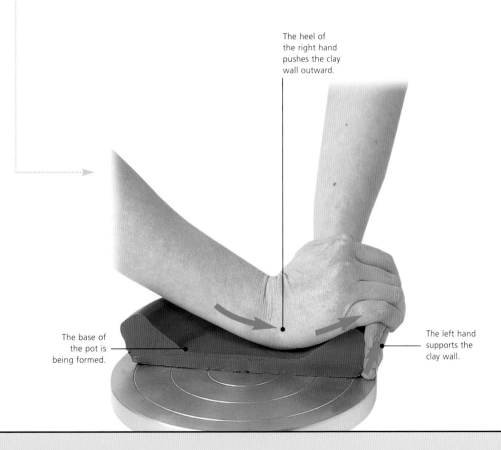

The heel of the right hand pushes the clay wall outward.

The base of the pot is being formed.

The left hand supports the clay wall.

A couple of slow, gentle lifts should be sufficient to create the height of the pot. Squeeze and consolidate the thick rim with the fingers and thumb of the left hand as the right hand gently presses down on it to further strengthen it. The walls of the pot should flare out a little, but remain fairly straight.

To create the roll foot, use a throwing rib against the bat to remove any excess clay. Then press the rounded corner of the rib into the wall of the pot just above the base. This creates a roll of clay at the base. Smooth the roll with the fingers. Use the rib to smooth the rest of the outer surface. Support the clay on the inside with the fingers of the left hand and gently press against the rib on the outside. Use the sharp corner of the rib to define the solid rim where it joins the pot. Mop out any excess water.

Remove the bat from the wheel with the pot and leave it to dry until just softer than leather hard. Remove the baking dish from the bat. It may need to be rewired to be moved easily. Place the pot on a new dry bat. To make the bowl oval, use a craft knife to cut a long, leaf-shaped piece of clay from the base. The wider the leaf, the narrower the dish. A little clay removed can make a big difference to the overall shape, so start with a small cut piece; the hole can always be made larger if necessary.

Place the hands flat against the walls of the pot and gently ease the walls inward. Do this slowly until the gap in the base closes and the two parts meet. If the pot grips the wooden bat, you may have to lift it up slightly to help push the base in.

5

6

7

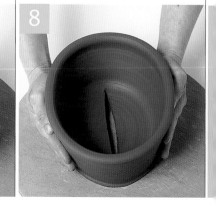

8

The right hand consolidates the clay in the thick rim.

The left thumb is on the outside of the pot, and the fingers on the inside.

The rib has smoothed the walls and is defining the rim.

The walls are of even thickness but a little heavier than on a normal bowl.

The clay walls have been squeezed, raised, and thinned.

The roll foot can clearly be seen.

The rim is left thick.

Use a wooden tool with a rounded end to press down on the join in the clay base to consolidate it. This will strengthen the join. Roll out a coil of clay and press this down into the join to fill in the hollow. Smooth the join with the fingers.

Use a kidney to finish the inside base. Scrape away any excess clay from the coil and smooth the join. Press down on the base again to create a good join and consolidate it. Use a little water to finally smooth the base. Leave the pot to dry a little before turning it over and smoothing the join on the bottom. Be careful not to push down too hard on the outside, as it may bow the base in.

As when any two pieces of clay are joined, the pot should be dried slowly before firing. This pot, if made correctly, will be able to withstand the thermal shock of being used in the oven. Being able to use the pottery we make to create other things, such as pies and flans, is part of the joy of pottery. It makes the whole experience all the more enjoyable and real. Many thrown forms can be altered and changed, so do not think of wheel-thrown pottery as always being round.

A knob hollowed out from the inside dries evenly: a thick, solid knob would dry very slowly and could explode if placed in the kiln while still damp on the inside.

A whole range of pots require lids to protect their contents. Storage jars are the most common.

The lid fits directly onto the gallery (a ridge designed for the lid to sit on).

The lip holds the lid in place.

Storage Jar

This tall storage jar is a basic cylinder shape enhanced by an interesting lid with an elaborate turned knob. The lid sits on a simple gallery. A series of jars of different heights with varied knobs would make an unusual and visually exciting kitchen set.

A vase-shaped jar with a cap lid is usually known as a ginger jar. This example has no knob, making it a very simple form to create. Without the knob, the lid is basically a small, flat-bottomed bowl inverted and placed on top.

The bread crock is the largest storage jar you are likely to need in the kitchen. This one has handles to help lift it, since they can be very heavy. The lid is much wider than on most storage vessels and has been kept simple. The barrel shape is very practical for storing loaves of bread; more complicated shapes could be impractical.

A lidded serving jug is a variation on the storage jar theme. The lid sits in the neck of the jug and a deep flange holds it in place. The lid would have to be removed to pour out the contents unless a pouring hole was cut into the flange, which could then be rotated to seal the jug.

A lid can be made in many different ways, though some consideration must be given to its practical function: does it have a good seal or can it be easily removed? Lids and knobs can also transform pots, giving visual interest as well as being practical. Aesthetically, matching pots to lids requires experimentation and practice to find what combinations work. Making lids is a challenge, as is getting them to fit. Pots and lids should be made at the same time and out of the same bag of clay, to prevent any variations in shrinkage, but accurate measuring is all-important.

This storage jar is made using 1 lb 8 oz (675g) of clay which should make a jar approximately 6 inches (15cm) high and 5 inches (13cm) wide when freshly made and still wet, and 11 oz (312g) to make the lid.

The walls are of similar thickness, tapering only slightly to the rim.

The beveled foot provides a line to glaze to.

KEY

⬅ Pulling, lifting, and shaping movements

⬅ Pushing, thickening, and supporting movements

Center the clay on the wheel (see pages 20–21). Push the thumb of the right hand into the center of the revolving clay. The wheel should be moving fairly swiftly and the hands and clay well lubricated. Push the thumb outward to open the hole further to create the base of the pot, supporting the wall with the left hand on the outside. The base of the pot should be tested with a pin at this stage to check its depth, as the pot will not be turned later. Press the thumb down on the base of the pot to consolidate the clay.

Place the thumb of the left hand at the base of the outside of the pot and the left fingers on the inside. Place your right hand on top of the clay wall and the left hand to provide support. Squeeze the clay between the fingers and thumb of the left hand to thin the clay. Pull this hand up the wall of the pot, squeezing as it goes, to further thin and raise the walls. Remember the vertical movement of the hand should be slower than the revolutions of the wheel. Leave the rim of the pot twice as thick as normal: this will be used to form the gallery (the ridge which the lid will sit on).

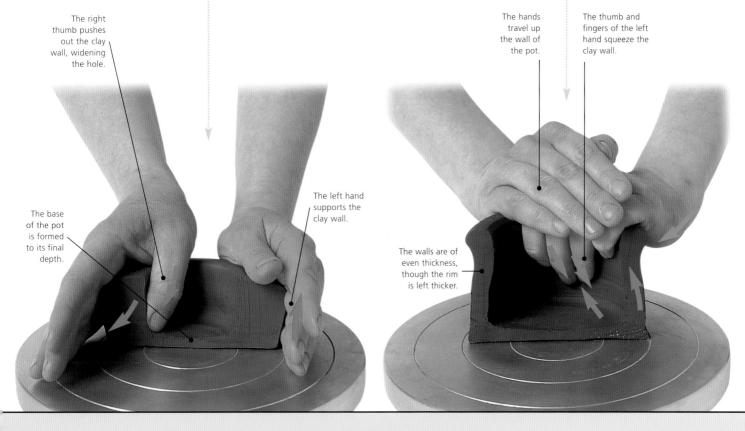

The right thumb pushes out the clay wall, widening the hole.

The base of the pot is formed to its final depth.

The left hand supports the clay wall.

The hands travel up the wall of the pot.

The thumb and fingers of the left hand squeeze the clay wall.

The walls are of even thickness, though the rim is left thicker.

While the pot is still short, place a downward pressure on the rim. Use the first finger of the left hand to push half the width of the rim downward on the inside, supporting the rim on the inside with the rest of the fingers of the left hand. Use the right hand over the left to support it and keep it steady. This action forms the ledge. Form the gallery slowly. Do not make it too deep or use too much of the rim as it may result in a thin wall that looks unfinished. You can use a throwing rib to form a sharper, more defined gallery.

The gallery and rim of the pot are now practically finished, so try not to touch them too much during the shaping of the rest of the pot. Shape and thin the walls of the pot further. Use the fingers of the left hand inside the pot to push out a bulge in the wall at the base, while supporting the neck with the left thumb. Place the knuckle of the right hand under the bulge on the outside and push it up the clay wall.

Continue to push out the bulge with the fingers of the left hand just ahead of the knuckle. Stop short of the rim and gallery. Lubricate the hands and clay, but keep the inside of the pot free from excess water. A couple of lifts should bring the storage jar to its full height, though you may require more. A little bit of the final curved shape has now been thrown into the body.

Use a throwing rib to smooth the surface of the storage jar and form the final profile. Press the clay wall against the rib from the inside using the fingers of the left hand. This should be done gently until confidence is built up. The body of the pot is slightly swelled, so push the form out from within and support it with the rib on the outside until you achieve a shape you are happy with. Do this slowly, as it is difficult to make the form thinner again once it has been widened.

The first finger of the left hand pushes half the width of the rim down to create the gallery.

The rest of the left fingers support the ledge from underneath. The right hand supports the left to prevent it from moving too much.

The pot walls still need to be thinned and shaped.

The walls are being thinned and shaped.

The left-hand thumb supports the neck of the storage jar.

The fingers of the left hand push out a bulge of clay.

The knuckle of the right hand pushes the bulge of clay up the wall.

The gallery of the pot will need to be refined since it may have been distorted slightly during the shaping process. Check that the gallery is perfectly round and not too shallow to hold the lid, or so deep as to make it difficult to remove the lid. Steady the rim with the right hand as the left fingers finish shaping the gallery. Use the rib to create a slight bevel under the base of the pot, using the point of the rib at an angle to remove a sliver of clay. This gives a line to glaze to and a guide for cutting wire under the pot.

Measure the width of the gallery with calipers. Leave the calipers set to this width; you will need this measurement to make the lid. Wire the pot, keeping the wire taut and completely flat with the wheel head as you pull it toward you. Place dry hands around the body of the pot and lift it upward. If it does not come away cleanly, wire it again and try once more. Try not to distort the pot, especially at the rim, otherwise the lid you are about to make may not fit properly. Place the pot on a dry bat.

To make the lid for this vessel, first center the ball of clay. Use both hands to form it into a tall cylinder. Press the right thumb halfway down inside the revolving clay. The very thick base will be used to turn the lid from later. Support the cylinder with the left hand, as such a tall, narrow form can easily start to wobble.

Place the thumb of the left hand at the base of the hole on the outside, halfway up the cylinder, and the fingers of the left hand on the inside. Place the right hand on top of the left to steady it. Squeeze the thumb and fingers of the left hand together to thin the clay. Use the squeezing action to draw the clay outward and upward to form a small, shallow bowl. Remember to lubricate the clay and hands when needed.

7

8

9

10

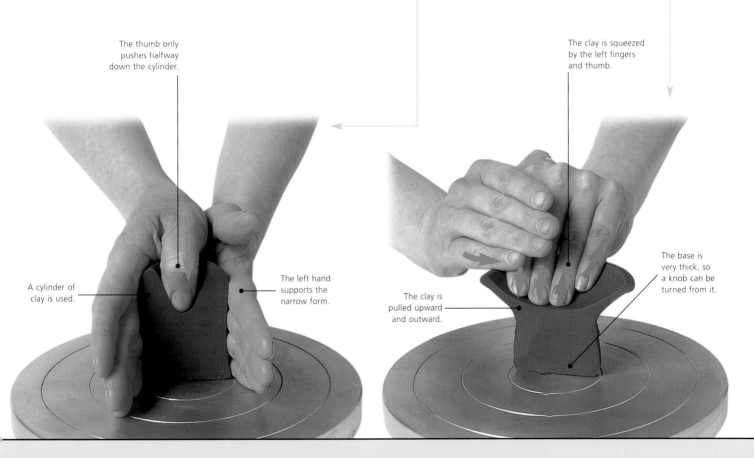

The thumb only pushes halfway down the cylinder.

A cylinder of clay is used.

The left hand supports the narrow form.

The clay is squeezed by the left fingers and thumb.

The clay is pulled upward and outward.

The base is very thick, so a knob can be turned from it.

Smooth the rim flat horizontally using the first finger of the right hand. Support underneath the lid with the remaining fingers of the left hand and use the right hand over the left to support it and keep it steady. This will create a flat surface for the lid to sit on inside the flat gallery and ensure a good fit. Check the width of the lid using the preset calipers. If the lid is too small, gently squeeze out the clay. If it is too big it can be turned away later. Wire the lid and remove it from the wheel. Leave to dry a little.

When the lid has dried a little, turn it over so the thick base that will form the knob can dry. When the lid is just slightly softer than leather hard (firm to the touch but still damp), it is ready to be turned on the wheel. Dampen the wheel and the rim of the lid. Place the lid in the middle of the wheel using the rings on the wheel head as a guide. Check that the lid is central. Stop the wheel and reposition the lid if necessary, remembering to dampen the rim. The lid will be held in place by suction.

Because there is more clay left than you need to form a knob, use a ribbon tool to remove the excess clay. Hold the tool in the right hand and rest the left hand on the lid, with the left thumb against the tool to hold it steady. The wheel should be moving fairly swiftly during turning as it is easier to turn with more speed. Have the shape of knob you want to create in mind (see pages 154–157), and form the clay into a general cylinder from which to turn it.

This knob has an undercut to make it easier to grip, so the clay has to be turned away to form this. Using the ribbon tool, slowly remove clay to form the knob (it is easier if the clay is a little softer than leather hard). Be careful not to remove too much at once, as it cannot be put back. The profile of the lid below the knob also needs to be decided on. This lid is curved underneath and so should be domed on the outside. Use the ribbon tool to remove clay to form this curve.

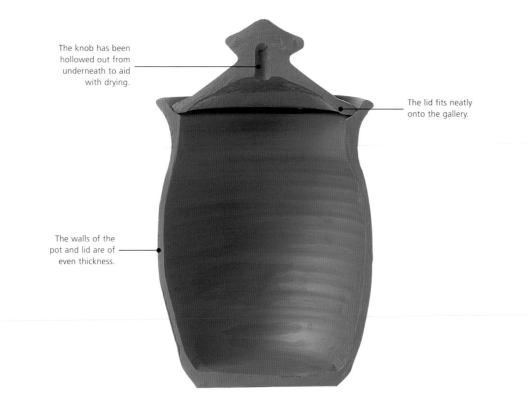

The knob has been hollowed out from underneath to aid with drying.

The lid fits neatly onto the gallery.

The walls of the pot and lid are of even thickness.

Finish by defining the shape. If the lid is slightly too big, use a craft knife to cut a sliver of clay away as the wheel rotates. Remove the lid from the wheel and check it in the gallery. If the body and lid are at different degree of dryness, they will shrink differently and later the lid may not fit. Before the lid is completely dry, use a hole-making tool to hollow out the knob from the inside to aid even drying and prevent it from exploding in the kiln.

This storage jar is quite simple, and many other shapes could be used to create all manner of variations. The lid could be made more complex using flanges to hold it in place and create a tighter seal. Storage jars are always useful and are needed in a variety of sizes, so practice making all types until you find one you enjoy making and like the look of. As long as the lids fit properly, then anything can be considered as a storage jar. Not all storage jars are functional for food; smaller ones can be made to hold jewelry or other small items.

101

Making a teapot is a process that utilizes all of the potter's skills— the culmination of those practiced in the more simple projects.

Teapot

A knob hollowed out from the inside dries evenly; a thick, solid knob would dry very slowly and could explode if placed in the kiln while still damp on the inside.

This hole lets air in to aid pouring and stop air locks that would cause the teapot to pour in spurts.

A very rounded teapot is particularly functional. The handle, which has been pulled on the pot and formed into a loop over the top, is the most noticeable feature. A handle like this would need to be dried very slowly as it may crack in the middle. The foot ring gives a spring to the form.

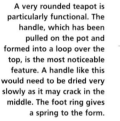

The body of this decorative teapot is based on a cone. Elaborate handles and knobs like this give the potter plenty to experiment with and develop an individual style.

The very high shoulder of this teapot gives it a refined shape. The spout needs to be placed quite high on the body to give balance. The lid is flush with the gallery, but still has flanges to keep it in place. The handle should be in proportion with the whole teapot form, so make sure it has the correct curve.

Two loops, to which a cane handle could be attached over the top of the body, replace the traditional ceramic handle. The lid very simply drops in. The shape is based on a simple cylinder and is very geometric. The spout tip has not been trimmed, which gives another interesting twist.

To make a teapot, three thrown elements must be fitted together, and a handle attached. You need to consider whether the spout will dribble, whether the lid will fall off during pouring, and if it is comfortable to hold and not too heavy when full of tea. It is always worth observing other handmade teapots to see what is possible, as teapots give a lot of scope for individuality in composition.

This teapot is made using 2 lb 8 oz (1.2kg) of clay for the body, 11 oz (312g) for the lid, and 11 oz (312g) for the spout, which should make a teapot, without its lid, approximately 6 inches (15cm) high and 4 inches (10cm) wide at the rim when still wet.

The spout is at the same height as the neck of the teapot.

The lid fits into the gallery neatly, while the flange hangs down into the pot so the lid does not fall out when the tea is poured.

The thumb can rest on this bump to aid the grip when the teapot is full.

All the elements have a similar thickness of clay.

KEY

⬅ Pulling, lifting, and shaping movements

⬅ Pushing, thickening, and supporting movements

Center the clay (see pages 20–21) and lubricate the clay and hands. Press the right thumb into the center of the clay. The wheel should be moving fairly swiftly. Push the thumb outward to widen the hole and form the base of the teapot, supporting the wall with the left hand on the outside. The base will not be turned, so check its thickness. Consolidate the clay at the base by pressing down with the right thumb. Because so many thermal strains are placed on teapots, it is important to make the pot strong.

Place the left thumb at the base of the teapot on the outside and the fingers of the left hand on the inside. Place the right hand on top of the clay wall and the left hand to provide support. Squeeze the thumb and fingers of the left hand together to thin the clay wall. While still squeezing, move the hand up the wall, thinning and raising the clay. Be careful to leave a wide rim of clay with which to form the gallery.

Use the left-hand fingers inside the pot to gently force out a bulge of clay just above the base. Place the knuckle of the right hand under the bulge on the outside and use it to push the bulge up the wall of the pot, as the wheel rotates a little slower. Use the left fingers to continue to push the bulge out, just above the rising knuckle. This thins and heightens the walls. Leave a rim twice as thick as normal to form the gallery. Lift the clay a couple of times to create a fairly cylindrical pot with a heavy rim.

Before you swell the body of the teapot, form the gallery. The cylindrical pot is strongest at this stage, and the downward pressure exerted on it could distort a thinner or wider form. Using the first finger of the left hand, push about half the thickness of the rim downward on the inside of the pot, supporting the rim on the inside with the rest of the fingers of the left hand. Use the right hand over the left to support and keep it steady. The rim and gallery are now at their final size, so try not to alter them in the following stages.

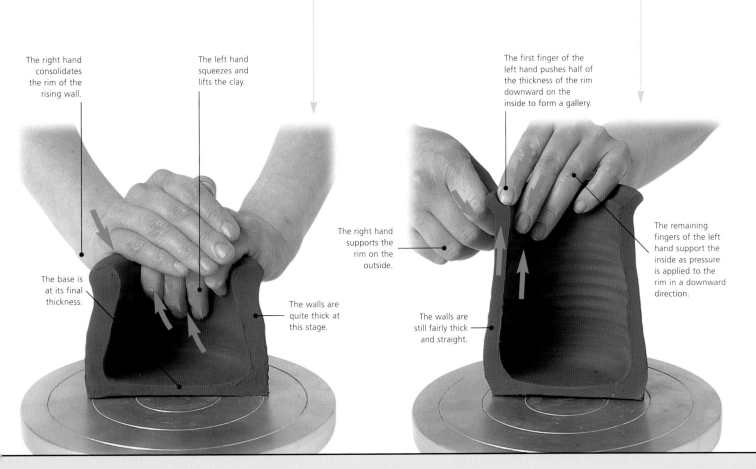

The right hand consolidates the rim of the rising wall.

The left hand squeezes and lifts the clay.

The base is at its final thickness.

The walls are quite thick at this stage.

The first finger of the left hand pushes half of the thickness of the rim downward on the inside to form a gallery.

The right hand supports the rim on the outside.

The remaining fingers of the left hand support the inside as pressure is applied to the rim in a downward direction.

The walls are still fairly thick and straight.

To swell the body of the teapot, lubricate the hands and clay. Push a bulge of clay out at the base with the left-hand fingers, and raise it with the right knuckle on the outside. Allow the belly to increase in diameter a little. Gently ease out the profile, taking care that it dosen't start to wobble. The wheel should be turning much slower now. The knuckle lift both thins the walls and creates the belly. Aim to have the widest part of the belly above the midpoint. A higher shoulder makes for a better looking form.

Define the final shape using a throwing rib. Smooth and compress the walls of the teapot by gently pushing the clay with the left fingers on the inside against the rib on the outside. Use the left thumb to support the rim.

During the shaping of the belly the gallery may have lost some of its clarity, so, using the fingers, define the profile again. If you find it easier to use the corner of the rib, place the rib in the right hand, push down and define the gallery while supporting it with the fingers of the left hand. Hold the flat edge of the rib on the spinning wheel and push it slightly under the base of the pot to form a sight bevel that provides a guide for the cutting wire and removes any excess clay.

The teapot body is now finished. Use calipers to measure the width of the gallery and make a note of this measurement to make the lid later. Wire under the base of the pot by keeping the wire taut and completely flat with the wheel head and pulling it toward you. Place clean, dry hands under the belly of the pot and lift it upward. If it is still stuck, wire it again. Put aside on a clean, dry bat. This is a relatively easy shape to pick up when wet, but do not to distort the neck.

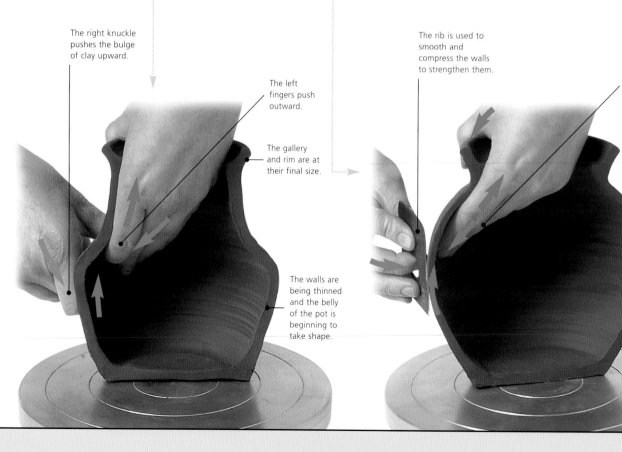

The right knuckle pushes the bulge of clay upward.

The left fingers push outward.

The gallery and rim are at their final size.

The walls are being thinned and the belly of the pot is beginning to take shape.

The rib is used to smooth and compress the walls to strengthen them.

The left hand pushes the clay against the rib and supports the neck.

The wall tapers slightly, which helps to support the wide body.

The spout is thrown and joined to the pot later. Center the ball of clay and push the thumb of the right hand into the center of the revolving clay. The spout does not need a base, so push the thumb right down to the wheel head. Support the wall with the left hand and push the right thumb outward to widen the hole.

Position the left thumb at the base of the pot on the outside and the fingers of the left hand on the inside. Place the right hand on top of the left hand to provide support. Squeeze and raise the left thumb and fingers upward to thin the clay and increase the height of the walls. Push inward as you lift to form a cone. Push out a bulge, a little way up from the base, from the inside with the fingers of the left hand, and lift it upward using the knuckle of the right hand on the outside.

With the fingers of both hands on the outside of the pot, push gently inward on the walls as you move your hands upward to narrow the form. This is called "collaring in." After doing this the clay wall will be thicker, so it may need to be thinned and raised again.

Using only one finger on the inside and a throwing rib on the outside, create the final shape of the spout. The walls of the spout need to be of even thickness to ensure that the tea will flow freely through it. Wire off the spout and leave to dry until leather hard.

9

10

11

12

The right hand supports the left and smooths the rising rim of the wall of clay.

The left thumb on the outside and the fingers on the inside squeeze and lift the clay upward.

The rib is used to smooth the profile of the spout.

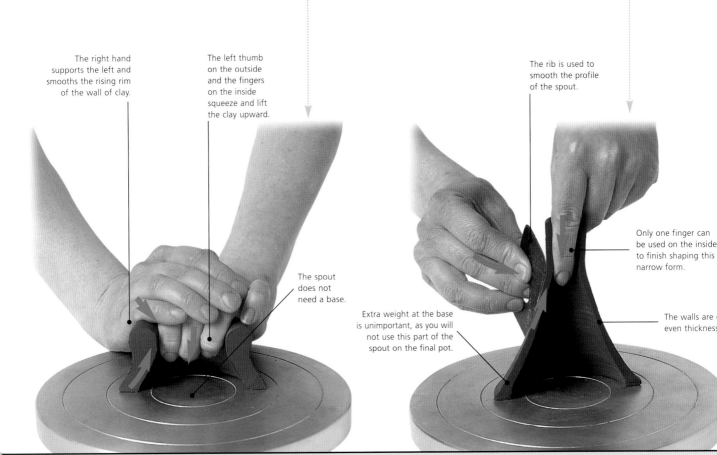

The spout does not need a base.

Only one finger can be used on the inside to finish shaping this narrow form.

Extra weight at the base is unimportant, as you will not use this part of the spout on the final pot.

The walls are of even thickness.

The lid is made upside down on the wheel and turned to its final shape later. Center the ball of clay into a narrower cylinder than normal. Push the thumb of the right hand only halfway down the depth of the revolving clay with the left hand supporting the clay wall. The bottom half of the ball of clay will form the knob during turning later.

To make a small bowl shape, position the left-hand thumb on the outside of the pot, the left fingers inside, and the right hand on top of the left. Squeeze the clay outward and upward between the left thumb and fingers.

The flange of the lid is now formed. This will ensure the lid does not tip off when the pot is poured. Use the little finger of the right hand to push the wall of the small bowl shape inward to form a ledge. Use one finger of the left hand on the outside of the pot and the others on the inside to support this shape as it is formed. Smooth the rim of the flange with one finger.

Set the calipers to the measurement previously taken of the top of the pot, and use them to measure the widest part of this form, the lip that sits in the gallery of the teapot base. Use the fingers to adjust the lid until it is the same size as the gallery. Check that the flange is narrow enough to drop inside the neck of the teapot. If the lid is marginally too big this can be turned and trimmed later when the knob is formed.

13

14

15

16

The right finger smooths the rim of the flange of the lid.

The ledge will sit on the gallery when the lid is in place.

The base is very thick and will be turned upside down and trimmed on the wheel to create a knob.

To help the lid stay in place you can, if you like, form a pouring lip in the flange. Without turning the wheel, gently smooth an area of the flange flat. Very gently squeeze as you flatten to thin the clay a little. Place the left thumb on one side of the flattened area and the first finger of the left hand on the other side. Gently squeeze the thumb and finger in a little. Lubricate the first finger of the right hand and, moving from side to side, gently ease the clay downward and bend the flange over to form the lip.

Wire the lid from the wheel, place to one side and allow it to dry a little. Then turn it over so the thick base that will form the knob can dry. When the lid is just slightly softer than leather hard it can be trimmed on the wheel. Dampen the wheel and the lid slightly and center the lid on the wheel. The lid will be held in place by suction. If the pouring lip was formed on the flange there will be no suction to hold the lid in place, so it will need to be held in place by three coils of clay placed under the ledge.

Use a ribbon tool to remove a lot of the excess clay. Hold the tool in the right hand and rest the left hand on the lid, with the left thumb against the tool to hold it steady. The wheel should be traveling fairly swiftly. Have in mind the style of knob you would like to create (see pages 154–157) and remember to leave enough clay to form it.

Remove clay until you have a general knob-shaped column left. If you need to make the lid narrower at its widest part to make it fit the teapot, remove a small amount of clay from the width of the lid at this stage. Check it by measuring with the calipers. It may be wise to remove it from the wheel and try it on the pot, but this means recentering the lid to finish turning the knob.

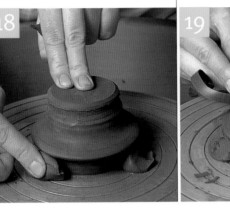

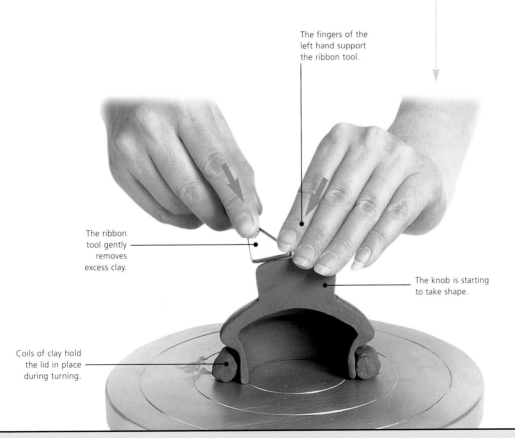

The fingers of the left hand support the ribbon tool.

The ribbon tool gently removes excess clay.

The knob is starting to take shape.

Coils of clay hold the lid in place during turning.

Use the ribbon tool to form the curve of the lid beneath the knob. It should be slightly domed so it follows the curve of the teapot body. This is difficult to visualize and only gets easier with practice. Knowing how much clay to remove eventually becomes second nature.

Use a variety of different shaped tools to form the final shape of the knob. This knob is designed to complement the simple, curved teapot shape. During the final touches the left hand holds the turning tool steady to prevent it slipping and destroying the profile of the knob.

The lid is now finished, except for a small hole that needs to be placed in the dome. Use a hole cutter to pierce the lid so that when the teapot is in use, air can flow into it as the tea flows out allowing it to pour smoothly. The knob of this lid is quite thick, so the hole cutter could be used to hollow out the knob from underneath, to help with even drying. Wire off the lid.

To attach the spout to the teapot body, both pieces need to be leather hard and of exactly the same dryness. Otherwise they may dry at different rates when joined, which can result in the spout cracking away from the body. Cut the spout from the cone using a craft knife at a diagonal angle to form a pouring spout. Alternatively, use a cutting wire to remove the spout from its base.

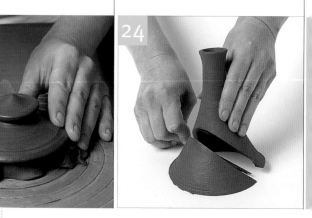

The knob has been hollowed out to aid with drying.

The knob is now turned away to its final shape.

The walls of the lid are of even thickness.

The vent hole has been made with a hole-making tool.

This lip in the flange will hook under the rim of the teapot.

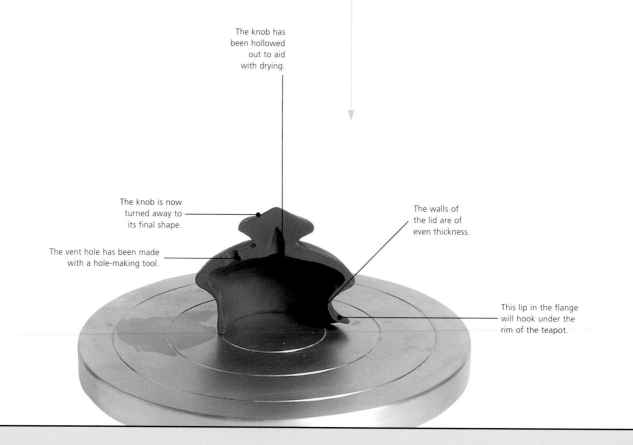

Use the knife to remove the thicker excess clay left at the base of the cone during throwing. You should have a pouring spout with walls of an even thickness. The spout can dry out quite quickly. If you find it is drier than the body, dip the widest part that will be attached to the pot in water to soften it slightly.

Place the spout where it looks most pleasing; here, it is placed on the widest part of the belly. If you are unsure about the position, press it on and stand back from the pot to assess the profile. When you are happy with the position, draw a line around it with the knife then remove it. Make sure the end of the spout is level with the gallery, or when hot water is poured into the pot it may flow out of the spout before the teapot is full.

Use the hole maker to bore holes into the center of the marked area. Create a symmetrical pattern of holes that will act as a strainer for the tea leaves or prevent the teabag blocking the spout. Just inside the outline of the spout position, use a craft knife to crosshatch all the way around. Crosshatch the edge of the spout as well. Place some slurry on the crosshatched area of the pot.

Place the spout over the strainer and press down evenly all the way around. You may want to support the wall of the teapot on the inside to prevent pushing the belly of the pot inward and distorting the form. Smooth the join as much as possible using the fingers and remove any excess slurry that has squeezed out of the join. Roll out a thin coil of clay and press this into the join all the way around the spout, blending until the join becomes seamless. Support the pot from the inside. Smooth with a sponge.

25

26

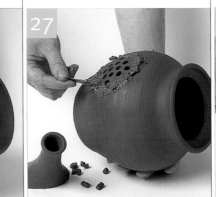

27

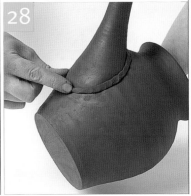

28

A spout positioned higher on the teapot body needs to be much shorter.

A spout positioned lower on the body needs to be much longer.

Tea poured from this pot will be weaker as the water is taken from the top of the teapot.

Tea poured from this spout will be stronger as it is coming from the bottom of the pot where the tea leaves are.

Make sure the end of the spout is about as high as the gallery. Using the knife, cut the clay at the end and trim the spout at an angle, being careful not to break it since it may be quite dry at its end by now. This forms a pouring hole with a larger area for better pouring.

Teapot spouts that are thrown "unwind" during firing. If the wheel rotates counterclockwise during throwing, as most Western wheels do, then the spout will unwind clockwise. Therefore, when you trim the spout you must allow for this by removing a little more clay from the left. Do this with the spout placed directly in front of you. The fired teapot spout will unwind and become straight.

Pull a handle from a coil of clay and let it dry a little (see pages 147–153). The handle needs to be wetter than the pot you are attaching it to so it can form a good curve without splitting. Crosshatch an area below the neck of the pot and dab on a little slurry. Take the handle in the right hand and bring it up to the pot. Pulled handles always taper slightly, so attach the wider end to the prepared area. Using the thumb of the left hand, smooth the join where the handle meets the pot.

Form the shape of the handle. It needs to be comfortable to hold and large enough to grip using the whole hand. Check the profile. When you are happy with the position and shape of the curved handle, use crosshatching and a little slurry to attach it about 2 inches (5cm) up from the base of the pot. This measurement is only approximate and you may feel a different position is better. The join can be filled with a small coil of clay to strengthen it if required.

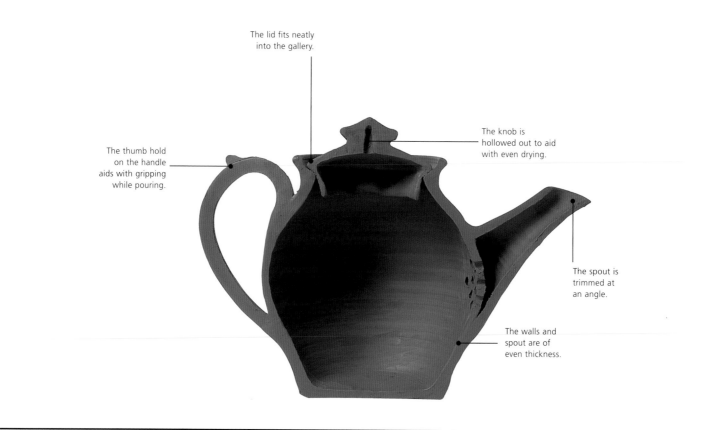

The lid fits neatly into the gallery.

The knob is hollowed out to aid with even drying.

The thumb hold on the handle aids with gripping while pouring.

The spout is trimmed at an angle.

The walls and spout are of even thickness.

To make pouring easier, a thumb hold can be placed on the top of the handle. This is a very small coil of clay smoothed onto the handle to form a bump. It forms a nice decorative feature as well as a practical point that helps prevent the teapot from slipping in the hand while in use. Wrap the whole pot loosely in plastic. This helps to slow the drying process and equalizes the moisture content of the various parts. This should prevent any of the joined parts from cracking or splitting apart.

This teapot is a traditional shape and design and is very practical to use. More elaborate lids and handles could be added to personalize this form. All manner of body shapes could be used to create teapots, and spouts can be shortened or elongated. Taller, more cylindrical shapes could be used to make coffee pots, which opens up another avenue to explore.

The joining of different thrown elements to create one cohesive form takes practice, but through experimentation and perseverance, teapots can become a potter's obsession and crowning glory.

Turning

When a pot is leather hard, that is stiff but still damp, it can be placed back on the wheel and turned, a process used to either remove unwanted clay that could not be removed during throwing to give a more refined and defined shape, or to create a foot ring—a raised base for the pot to stand on. Turning can also be used to create a variety of surface textures and finishes.

Tools for turning need to be sharp, otherwise they may not cut the clay easily. If too much force is used to remove clay, then the shape of the pot could easily be distorted.

The consistency of the clay is also very important. Eventually you will find a state of dryness that best suits you. Every potter's description of "leather hard" varies. Some potters turn their pots while they are quite soft, others prefer them to be slightly harder than leather hard. If the clay is too dry, however, the tool may skip over the the pot's surface or cause irregular marks called "chattering."

Turning refines pots. Some pottery looks best left alone, while other forms benefit from turning. It depends on what finished result you are trying to achieve. Do not turn just for the sake of it.

Fixing pots in position for turning

When a thrown pot reaches the leather-hard stage, it can be replaced on the wheel, centrally and often upside down, and turned to remove excess clay and define its shape (see pages 120–121).

Some pots can simply be placed on a damp wheel head and will stay in place with the help of suction. Others will need to be secured using coils of clay around the rim. Alternatively, chucks can be used to support a pot, keeping it central

A chuck for a bowl

method 1
Center a large, thick coil of clay on the wheel. Using a little water, throw the ring until it is smooth and even, applying downward pressure to consolidate the clay.

Using a pair of calipers, measure the inside width of the bowl's rim and check that the outside width of the chuck is the same. It is always best to make chucks a little on the large side because they can easily be trimmed with a ribbon tool (see pages 118–119). If you have a few bowls to turn, start with the biggest and trim away parts of the same chuck to fit the smaller bowls each time. Leave the chuck to dry until it is stiff. If it is too damp it may stick to the bowl.

Place the upside down, leather-hard bowl over the chuck. The bowl is now locked and secured in position for turning. Because the chuck is centered, the bowl placed over it should also be automatically centered.

The chuck is centered on the wheel.

The chuck is the same width as the inside of the pot and holds it securely in position.

The chuck can be re-used to turn other bowls of a similar width.

and preventing damage to its rim, and it is difficult to successfully smooth or repair a damaged rim. The rim of the pot and its roundness are the first things your eye falls on, so damage caused to fragile rims by sticking them directly to the wheel head can be very noticeable.

The use of a chuck also speeds up the process if a set of pots needs turning, as the same chuck can be reused, and recentering is not required.

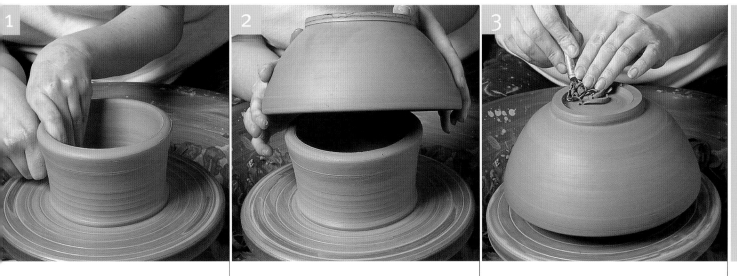

method 2
Throw a cylinder of clay (see pages 24–27), without a base, that is deeper than the bowl. Leave the chuck to dry until it is stiff. If it is too damp it may stick to the bowl or collapse, however it should remain slightly damper than the bowl so that it does not slip off. Dampen it with a sponge if necessary. This chuck could be thrown on a wooden bat (see page 35). If the chuck on the bat were wrapped in plastic it could be reused almost indefinitely.

Using a pair of calipers, measure the inside width at the base of the bowl and check that the outside width of the chuck is the same measurement. Center the upside down, leather-hard bowl over the chuck, then spin the wheel to check, and adjust if necessary.

The bowl is held in place by gravity and friction, but you should support it with the left hand opposite the ribbon tool to spread the force being applied to it. The advantage of this chuck is that pressure can be put on the base of the pot to turn a deep foot ring without the fear of distorting or breaking the rim because the rim is suspended in mid air. The form can be easily turned because it is not obscured by coils of clay.

The chuck supports the bowl away from the wheel.

The rim does not touch the wheel so should not get damaged.

A chuck for a vase

If the neck of a vase is too weak or narrow to support the weight of the rest of the pot during turning, a chuck must be used.

A chuck for a bottle

A bottle form has a long neck that cannot support the body of the pot during turning. Bottles are also often a little tall for a thrown chuck, so a prefired pot is used instead. This chuck can be used to hold a variety of forms, from vases to bowls, during turning, and one main advantage is that you do not have to wait for the chuck to dry. Any shape of prefired pot that suits the shape and size of the pot being turned can be used. For very large pots, buckets can be used, and for the very small, try eggcups.

1 Throw a cylinder with straight walls (see pages 24–27), without a base, that is wide enough to place the rim of the vase inside but narrow enough to support the shoulder of the pot. Leave the chuck to dry until it is stiff. If it is too damp it may stick to the vase or collapse under its weight. This chuck could be thrown on a wooden bat (see page 35).

2 While turning, support the vase with the left hand on the opposite side to the ribbon tool to spread the pressure being applied to it and prevent the vase pushing down into the chuck and being sent unevenly off center. Place the rim of the leather-hard vase inside the chuck, making sure the base is completely flat and central. Spin the wheel to check. It may look central and flat until it is rotated.

1 Choose a tall, narrow fired pot that is wide enough to support the shoulder of the bottle, but tall enough for the length of the neck not to touch the bottom on the inside. Place this pot centrally on the wheel and use three coils of clay to hold it in position.

2 Place a coil of clay around the neck of the pot and push it firmly on. Try to make this coil as even and round as possible, using your fingers to smooth it. Use plenty of clay, since this coil provides a cushion for the pot to rest on; a soft pot placed directly onto the fired pot would easily be marked. Spin the wheel and gently smooth the upper surface of the coil.

3 Use a craft knife to trim the inside of the coil, making sure the inside profile of this chuck is centered. Use both hands to hold the knife still and cut gently downward to remove any uneven clay. If the rim is very uneven it can also be trimmed with the knife. No water has been used to make this chuck, so it only takes a short while to stiffen before it can be used.

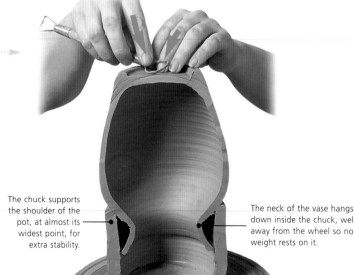

The chuck supports the shoulder of the pot, at almost its widest point, for extra stability.

The neck of the vase hangs down inside the chuck, well away from the wheel so no weight rests on it.

A chuck for a plate

Plates are wide and shallow and need support in the middle of their bases to prevent them from being pushed in as turning progresses.

Place the leather-hard bottle upside down in the neck of the chuck, which will support it at its shoulder where it is almost at its widest, providing maximum support during turning. Check the bottle is centered by spinning the wheel. Reposition it until it rotates smoothly and there is no wobble or undulation.

While turning, use the left hand opposite the ribbon tool to support the bottle. Do not apply too much pressure too suddenly, as it may destabilize the whole assembly and knock it off-center. Rotate the wheel at a medium speed. When turning is finished, the bottle is easily lifted out of the chuck. The chuck can be reused if required.

Center a piece of clay (see pages 20–21) and throw a circle that is as deep as the inside of the plate, so the rim of the plate touches the wheel head but the center of the base is supported by the chuck. Leave the chuck to dry until it is stiff. If it is too damp it may stick to the plate. This chuck could be thrown on a wooden bat (see page 35).

Place the upside down, leather-hard plate over the chuck and check to see if it is central by spinning the wheel. You may need to push it slightly to correct its position. If the rim is very fragile or decorative, it should not touch the wheel. A much deeper chuck could be thrown, which would raise the plate away from the wheel. Re-centering with a deeper chuck would be more difficult, but not impossible.

While turning, any pressure applied to the base of the plate will be supported by the chuck, but try to limit the amount of downward force used, as it is not foolproof, and the base could still be distorted slightly.

The rim of the plate touches the wheel head for extra stability, but this is not always desirable.

The turning tool applies pressure to the base of the plate that is supported from underneath by the chuck.

Turning simple bases

These vases need to be turned to remove excess weight left during the throwing process. Turning will result in a more refined shape.

Curved vase

This curved vase is turned the right way up mainly because it has a narrow, delicate neck that would probably not be able to support its own weight if it were turned upside down. The profile of this vase has been greatly improved by turning away the extra clay at its base. As your throwing improves, this kind of turning will not be necessary.

Dampen the base of the vase and the wheel head and position the vase centrally on the wheel (see pages 114–117). Using a triangular turning tool, begin to trim away the excess clay at the base of the pot. Support the pot with the left hand to prevent it flying off the wheel, and hold the tool in the right hand. Place the flat side of the tool against the wall of the pot and begin to trim the clay away by pushing the tool downward.

Push the extra clay down and away from the pot. This pot is softer than leather hard. If it were dryer, the extra clay cutaway would break up as it was removed. It is a matter of personal preference as to what dryness you turn your pots at. Continue to remove clay from the base until you achieve the desired profile. Be careful to match it to the inside profile; if the walls are made too narrow at the base, you may weaken the pot. Turn a bevel into the base to give the pot a finishing point that stops it from looking heavy at the base. Remove the vase from the wheel head and allow to dry.

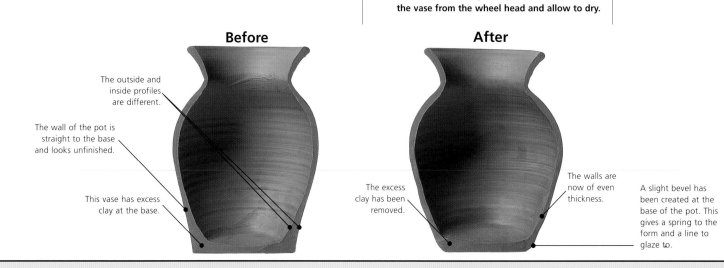

Before

The outside and inside profiles are different.

The wall of the pot is straight to the base and looks unfinished.

This vase has excess clay at the base.

After

The excess clay has been removed.

The walls are now of even thickness.

A slight bevel has been created at the base of the pot. This gives a spring to the form and a line to glaze to.

Straight vase

This vase has a wide neck, so it can be turned upside down because it is unlikely to misshape or be weakened during the turning process. This straight vase is very practical and could have many uses. Turning is often used as a way of removing unevenness until your throwing technique improves, though the underneath of this vase is improved only by turning.

Dampen the rim of the pot and the wheel head and place the vase upside down centrally on the wheel head (see pages 114–117). Suction should hold it in place, but use sausages of clay around the rim for extra support if you prefer. Begin to turn away the excess clay from the base of the wall with a ribbon tool. Hold the tool in the right hand and rest the left hand on the pot with the left thumb against the tool to hold it steady. The wheel should be traveling fairly swiftly. Turning is much easier if the wheel moves quickly because less pressure is required to remove slivers of clay.

The sides of this vase should be straight, so trim clay from the width of the base. Then create a bevel by changing the angle of the ribbon tool to remove slightly more clay at a steeper angle. This narrows the base and gives a visible lift to the pot, as well as a line to glaze to. One advantage of being able to turn a pot upside down is that the base can also be trimmed using a ribbon tool. Use the ribbon tool to make the base slightly concave, then only the outside rim of the base wall will touch the table and the vase is less likely to wobble. Remove the vase from the wheel head and allow to dry.

Before   ## After

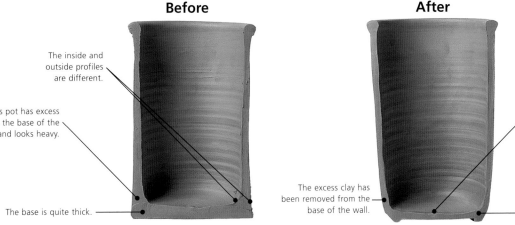

The inside and outside profiles are different.

This pot has excess clay at the base of the wall and looks heavy.

The base is quite thick.

The excess clay has been removed from the base of the wall.

The base has been trimmed to make it thinner and to create a very shallow foot ring, so only the outside edge touches the table.

A bevel has been cut into the base to lighten and finish the form.

Turning foot rings

Turning a foot ring allows you to remove excess clay, and creates a raised pedestal for a pot to stand on.

Straight-sided concealed foot ring

Foot rings are not always obvious; this one is concealed under the pot and its main purpose is to remove excess weight from the bottom of the pot.The foot ring is concealed under the pot and isn't part of its overall decorative nature. It serves to lift the pot up off the table and make it less likely to wobble, and a little lighter.

1

2

3

When the pot is leather hard, feel the base with your fingers to gauge the amount of clay that can be safely removed: test this with a pin. Place the pot upside down centrally on the wheel (see pages 114–117). Tuck your elbows into your body to help hold your hands still. Use a ribbon tool, held in your right hand, to tidy up the outside base and create a defined bevel. The left hand also touches it to give support and to stop the tool from making any sudden movements that may remove large chunks. The wheel should be traveling fairly swiftly. Turning is much easier if the wheel moves quickly because less pressure is required to remove clay.

Use the ribbon tool to remove excess clay from the base of the pot. Smooth the whole base first by removing a thin layer of clay to ensure that it is completely flat.

Use the ribbon tool to cut the foot ring into the base, leaving a ring on the outside. Begin to remove clay from inside this area. Be careful not to dig too deep or you may go right through the base. Remove only small amounts of clay at a time, until the right depth of foot ring is achieved. Remove the pot from the wheel head and allow to dry upside down.

Before

After

A little clay removed from the outside of the pot will also improve its shape.

This pot has a very heavy base that requires turning.

The excess clay has been removed from the outside base and a clear bevel created.

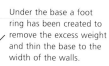

Under the base a foot ring has been created to remove the excess weight and thin the base to the width of the walls.

Standard foot ring on a rounded profile

Foot rings are often turned on rounded bowl forms because it is difficult to achieve a narrow face while throwing, since the extra clay is needed at the base to support the wide form. The foot ring on this bowl is decorative as well as functional. Bowls that do not have foot rings can look very heavy and unfinished.

1

When the bowl is leather hard, position it upside down centrally on the wheel head (see pages 114–117). Hold a ribbon tool in the right hand and rest the left hand on the pot, with the left thumb against the tool to keep it steady. Use the ribbon tool to begin to remove clay from the width of the base. There is quite a lot of clay to remove, so don't be too cautious. The wheel should be traveling fairly swiftly.

2

When the desired width of base is achieved, use the ribbon tool in the same way to define the outside profile of the foot. Here it is rounded, which on such a round bowl continues the design.

3

Remove the inside of the foot using the ribbon tool to build up a foot ring. On a thick base like this lots of clay has to be removed. Remember to leave the width of the foot ring and do not make it too thin or it will be all too easy to damage. When the correct depth is turned away, smooth the base of the foot ring with a flat tool to iron out any bumps or irregularities. The base of the pot, inside the foot ring, should follow the inside curve of the bowl, so it will be deeper nearer the foot ring. Remove the pot from the wheel head and allow to dry upside down.

Before

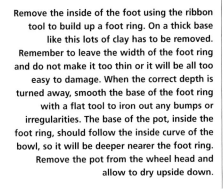

Excess clay has been left at the base to support the clay wall during throwing.

The base has been purposefully left thick to form a foot ring from.

After

The inside and outside of the pot follow the same shape, and the wall and base are of an even thickness.

The foot ring has a curved profile.

Excess clay at the base has been removed.

Foot ring on a shallow dish

This bowl is low and wide and needs a particular shape of foot ring to complement its form. This bowl is a useful serving dish. The foot ring gives the whole form a visual lift and helps us to see under the bowl. Without it, the dish would be almost flat to the table.

1 Place the leather-hard pot upside down centrally on the wheel head (see pages 114–117). A chuck could be used to support this form if you prefer. Begin to trim away excess clay from the width of the base with a flat-sided ribbon tool. Hold the tool in the right hand and rest the left hand on the pot, with the left thumb against the tool to hold it steady. The wheel should be traveling fairly swiftly; turning is much easier if the wheel moves quickly because less pressure is required to remove slivers of clay.

2 When you are happy with the outside profile, start to form a foot ring profile that is angular and a similar shape to the bowl. This foot ring is quite deep, so lots of clay needs to be removed from inside it. Support the tool with the left hand and rest your arms on the wheel tray to hold them still. Take the base down so that it is the same thickness as the walls. If you are unsure about the thickness you can remove the bowl and check it with your fingers, but you will need to recenter the bowl before you can continue turning.

3 Smooth the base of the foot ring with a flat tool to remove any lumps or unevenness. Remove the pot from the wheel head and allow to dry upside down.

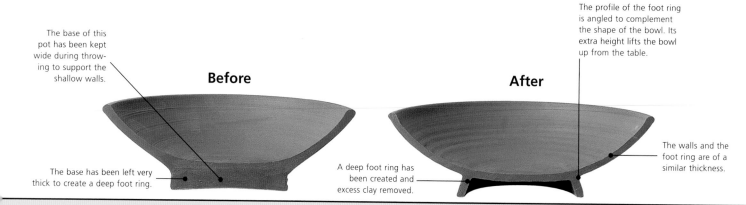

The base of this pot has been kept wide during throwing to support the shallow walls.

Before

The base has been left very thick to create a deep foot ring.

The profile of the foot ring is angled to complement the shape of the bowl. Its extra height lifts the bowl up from the table.

After

A deep foot ring has been created and excess clay removed.

The walls and the foot ring are of a similar thickness.

Two foot rings on a wide-based plate

A large plate often requires two foot rings to support its wide base during firing to prevent sagging. The base of the plate has remained flat during firing due to the support of the extra foot ring. The plate is quite light because a lot of clay was removed during turning.

This plate is wider than the wheel head so must be placed on a wooden bat (see page 35). It is advisable to use a chuck under the middle of the base of the plate to prevent it from sagging while turning (see pages 114–117). Use a ribbon tool to remove the excess clay from the walls of the plate. Hold the tool in the right hand and rest the left hand on the plate and use it to steady the tool. The wheel should be traveling fairly swiftly. Define the shape of the foot. It is a small, short vertical wall. Plates do not normally have decorative feet, as they are so low to the table that you don't see them.

Use the ribbon tool to remove clay around what will be the first foot ring circle, just outside the center of the plate. Hold the flat tool with boths hands, and gently rest it on the foot ring holding it very still. This first foot ring will support the center of the plate during drying and firing to prevent it from sagging. The foot ring is a simple band of clay left behind.

Form the outside foot ring at the edge of the plate base and remove the excess clay between the two. The second foot ring is about the same thickness as the first. Gently smooth the base of the foot rings to remove any bumps, but be careful not to remove too much clay. If you do, they may end up at different heights, which will cause the plate to rock or wobble. Remove the pot from the wheel head and allow to dry upside down.

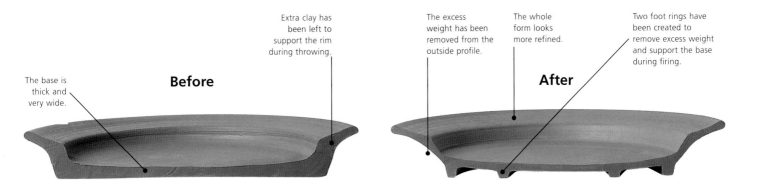

The base is thick and very wide.

Extra clay has been left to support the rim during throwing.

Before

The excess weight has been removed from the outside profile.

The whole form looks more refined.

Two foot rings have been created to remove excess weight and support the base during firing.

After

Altering a foot ring to create three feet

Once foot rings have been created, they can be altered and cut into to explore new ideas. Using the foot ring has advantages over adding separate feet. Being an integral part of the pot, it is unlikely to crack away from it as it dries.

Three feet, evenly spaced apart, will stop a pot from wobbling or rocking, even if one of them is shorter. If you try to make four feet and one distorts, then the pot may be unsteady. Many different designs could be made this way to create pots with interesting bases.

1
Place the bowl centrally upside down on the wheel head (see pages 114–117). Remove excess clay from the width of the base using a ribbon tool. Hold the tool in the right hand and rest the left hand on the pot, with the left thumb against the tool to steady it. The wheel should be traveling fairly swiftly; turning is much easier if the wheel moves quickly because less pressure is required to remove slivers of clay.

2
Use the ribbon tool to roughly shape the outside profile of the foot before removing the extra clay from the base. There is a lot of clay to be removed and the foot ring is quite deep.

3
The inside curve of the base should follow the outside curve of the walls. While turning away the base, try to visualize the bowl without the foot ring to see the outside curve. Remove the pot from the wheel head and allow to dry upside down.

Before

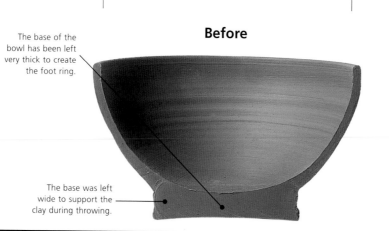

The base of the bowl has been left very thick to create the foot ring.

The base was left wide to support the clay during throwing.

Measure around the foot ring and divide it up into three sections. Mark out the positions for the three feet with a craft knife, each mark about 1 inch (2.5cm) long.

To create the feet, use a craft knife to make vertical cuts down through the foot ring. Begin to remove the unwanted sections of clay by cutting through the foot ring at its base at the same angle as the wall of the pot. Continue until the three larger sections have been removed.

Smooth away any ridges of clay that are left between the three feet with the side of a knife and finish with a sponge. Remove the pot from the wheel and allow to dry upside down so you do not accidentally damage the feet.

After

The excess clay has been removed from the outside profile of the base.

The inside profile of the pot follows exactly the outside curve and extends under the base.

The foot ring splays out a little to create a good shape from which to create individual feet.

The base is now hollow.

Throwing foot rings

Another way to create a foot ring is to place a coil or ball of clay on the base of a recentered, upside down pot and throw it, creating a raised base. This is useful if the base was not left deep enough to turn a foot ring when originally thrown, or if you want a more elaborate foot ring.

Wide foot ring

This is quite a deep foot ring and, if it was to be turned, a lot of clay would have to be left during throwing to form it. This foot ring is like a short pedestal that lifts the bowl up off the table.

1	2	3	4

Position a leather-hard, firm to the touch but still damp, bowl centrally upside down on the wheel head (see pages 114–117). Use a craft knife to crosshatch the area where the foot ring will be attached, forming a key that allows the new clay to grip to the pot. Roll a coil of clay out evenly, ready to be thrown.

Press the coil of clay evenly onto the crosshatched area. Carefully dampen the coil and lubricate the hands. Try not to use too much water as the leather-hard pot will quickly absorb it and may begin to soften. Spin the wheel slowly and begin to smooth the coil of clay with the fingers.

To throw the clay coil, position the fingers of the left hand on the inside of the coil and the left thumb on the outside base of the coil. Use the right hand on top of the left hand to support it. Squeeze together the left fingers and thumb to make the coil an even thickness. Push the side of the right hand firmly down on the rim to compress the clay. You are centering the coil of clay and making it even. The join between the ring and the bowl can be smoothed either with the fingers or a curved corner of a throwing rib.

Once the clay is even, increase the height of the coil to form a wall. This is quite a deep foot ring, so raise the wall upward by squeezing it between the fingers and thumb of the left hand. If the rim of the foot ring is uneven it can be trimmed with a pin. When the correct shape has been achieved, remove the bowl from the wheel. Leave it to dry upside down until the thrown foot has stiffened. When it has, cover loosely with plastic to help the pot's moisture content equalize, which will prevent the wetter foot from cracking away from the pot.

Pedestal base

This pedestal springs organically from the bowl, as no feature is made of the join. The flowing curves complement one another. A foot ring like this would be virtually impossible to turn from a solid base.

Place a leather-hard pot upside down centrally on the wheel head. It is a good idea to use a chuck under the center of the bowl (see pages 114–115) because a lot of pressure may be exerted here. Use a craft knife to cross-hatch the center of the base and press a fairly large ball of clay down onto it. Lubricate the clay and your hands with water, but try to keep the water to a minimum.

You are now going to, in effect, throw another pot. Center the ball of clay (see pages 20–21), but try not to exert too much downward pressure. Use the right thumb to open the clay and push a wall of clay outward, supporting the wall with the left hand on the outside. The thumb needs to go down as far as the base of the pot. You will know when it is deep enough, as the pot is harder than the clay you are throwing.

Slowly raise the wall by squeezing the clay between the left fingers on the inside and the left thumb on the outside. To make a pedestal this tall, a couple of lifts will be required. Rest the right hand on top of the left and on the rim of the pedestal for support. Little water should be used during this process. The pedestal will look best if it is wider at the top and narrower where it joins the pot. Make sure that the part that will touch the table is smooth and nicely rounded.

Once the wall is high enough, smooth it with a throwing rib by pushing the clay onto the rib from inside the pot with the left fingers. This will compress and strengthen the new pedestal. Smooth the base where it joins the bowl so it all becomes the same form. Remove the bowl and pedestal from the wheel head and let them dry upside down until the thrown pedestal has stiffened. Cover loosely with plastic to help the pot's moisture content equalize, which will prevent the wetter pedestal from cracking away from the bowl.

Narrow foot rings

These finished pots show the effect that different foot rings can have on the same bowl. Foot rings can be elaborate or simple, tall or shallow. The technique of throwing foot rings opens up new possibilities that could not be easily turned. When these foot rings are leather hard, they could be recentered and turned if sharper edges or shapes were required (see page 121), as throwing directly does have its limitations.

design 1
Position a leather-hard, firm to the touch but still damp, bowl centrally upside down on the wheel head (see pages 114–117). Use a craft knife to crosshatch an area on the base. Push a small ball of clay onto the center of the bowl where the crosshatching will grip the soft clay. Lubricate the hands and clay with a little water, but try to keep this to a minimum to avoid the leather-hard pot soaking up too much liquid.

Open out a small piece of clay using the first finger of the right hand rather than the thumb. Draw the finger toward your body to open the clay further while the left hand supports the clay wall.

To create a low, wide foot, draw the clay out as you raise it. Support the clay on the inside with two fingers of the left hand and use the forefinger of the left hand to steady the rim. You can also use the little finger to smooth the join between the bowl and the foot while the left fingers press the join on the inside to ensure a strong union. Remove the bowl from the wheel. Leave to dry upside down, until the foot ring has stiffened, then cover it loosely with plastic to equalize the moisture content, which will prevent the wetter foot ring from cracking away from the pot.

This variation is a little more elaborate, and turns the same bowl into a more elegant and refined form.

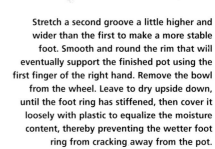

design 2
Repeating step 1 on page 128, push a small ball of clay onto the center of the bowl where the crosshatching will grip the soft clay. Lubricate the hands and clay with a little water, but try to keep this to a minimum. Center the ball of clay on the base of the pot, but try to avoid using too much downward pressure. Keep the clay ball small and narrow and in the center of the bowl. Push your right thumb into the center of the revolving clay to open it, while supporting the clay wall with the left hand. Push down until the thumb meets the base of the bowl. Support your arms on the edge of the wheel tray, to help keep them steady.

Raise the wall of the foot ring a little. With the left thumb on the outside and the left fingers on this inside, raise the wall by squeezing thumb and fingers together and lifting upward as the wheel rotates. Leave the wall fairly thick, as the decoration you will form with your fingers is quite deeply grooved. Support the clay on the inside with two fingers of the left hand and use the forefinger of the left hand to steady the rim. Use the little finger of the right hand to push a groove into the clay wall near the base of the foot ring. Use either fingers or the rounded corner of a ribbon tool to smooth the join between the ring and the bowl.

Stretch a second groove a little higher and wider than the first to make a more stable foot. Smooth and round the rim that will eventually support the finished pot using the first finger of the right hand. Remove the bowl from the wheel. Leave to dry upside down, until the foot ring has stiffened, then cover it loosely with plastic to equalize the moisture content, thereby preventing the wetter foot ring from cracking away from the pot.

Throwing and joining a separate foot ring

It is possible to throw a foot ring separately and join it to the pot when they are both leather hard, or just softer. If the two pieces are of the same dryness when joined, less pressure is put on the bowl than if the foot ring were directly thrown onto the base. A range of different bases can be made and tried for suitability before joining, giving you more control over the final result. These bowls are identical, apart from the attached foot rings that alter the whole profile and height of the finished pots. It can be difficult to visualize parts of pots that are made separately until they are joined, and it takes a little practice to know what will look good and work proportionately. It is perfectly acceptable to make a few different foot rings to try out, and only use the best.

1	2	3	4

1 Center a small ball of clay on the wheel (see pages 20–21). Push the thumb of the right hand into the center of the clay right down to the wheel head, as this foot ring has no need of a base. Push outward with the thumb while supporting the clay wall with the left hand. Lubricate the hands and clay with water as needed.

2 Thin the walls and define the shape. With the left thumb on the outside and the left fingers on this inside, raise the wall by squeezing thumb and fingers together and lifting upward as the wheel rotates. The foot ring is thrown upside down, so the highest part will be what touches the table, while the untidy part that is at the wheel head will be attached to the pot. Leave the rim of this foot ring a little heavier so it is a sturdy support for the finished pot. Wire the foot ring from the wheel, keeping the wire taut and completely flat with the wheel head, and pull it toward you. Let it dry until it is almost leather hard.

3 For a more elaborate foot ring, squeeze the clay upward between the fingers of the left hand on the inside of the pot and the left thumb on the outside. With the right hand over the left to support it, form a fairly narrow cylinder. The fingers can be pressed into the outside of the wall to shape it, creating concentric rings of clay to produce a decorative finish. There is a limit to the shapes that fingers alone can make, but various tools could be used to form, for example, sharper edges. When you are happy with the shape, wire the foot ring carefully from the wheel and leave to dry a little.

4 Center a leather-hard bowl upside down on the wheel (see pages 114–117). Crosshatch an area on the base of pot and add a little slurry. Position the foot ring over the cross-hatched area. The two pieces should be of the same consistency when they are joined so they will shrink at the same rate. Make sure the foot ring is centrally positioned, then press it firmly into position. Smooth the join with the little finger to remove any excess slurry and to compress the join. This foot ring has a definite shape where it meets the pot, so be careful not to misshape it. Remove the pot from the wheel head and leave to dry upside down until the join has set

Throwing and joining a separate pedestal

A pedestal could be considered to be a very large foot ring, and it is often easier to make one as a separate piece that can be joined later. This pedestal bowl has a fairly simple design, but all kinds of shapes could be achieved using the same technique. Throwing this complete shape at one time and turning the pedestal would be impossible, so this is a useful way of creating new designs by joining two different parts together to make a whole.

1 A pedestal is basically a cylinder vase and so requires quite a lot of clay. Center the clay on the wheel (see pages 20–21) and open it out with the thumb of the right hand. Push the thumb through right to the wheel head, as this pedestal has no need of a base. Use the thumb to push the clay wall outward while supporting the wall from the outside with the left hand. Lubricate the hands and clay with water as needed. Squeeze the clay between the left thumb on the outside and the left fingers on the inside and raise the wall. Use the right hand over the left to support it.

2 A pedestal this tall may require a knuckle lift to get it to its full height. Support the clay wall on the inside with your left hand as the fingers of the right hand push into the base of the pot to create a bulge of clay. Place the knuckle of the right hand under this bulge and keep the left hand inside the bulge just above the knuckle on the outside. Lift the bulge of clay up the side of the pot against the fingers of the left hand. Leave the rim fairly thick, as this will eventually become the base of the whole form. Carefully wire the pedestal from the wheel, and leave to dry a little.

3 Center the bowl upside down on the wheel (see pages 114–117). Use a craft knife to crosshatch an area on the base of the pot and the base of the pedestal. Use a little slurry to stick the two parts together.

4 Check that the pedestal is positioned centrally on the bowl. Tall additions like this are more likely to wobble or be slightly off center, although, as long as this is not too extreme, a little movement is acceptable. Push the two parts gently but firmly together. Spin the wheel and smooth the join. Remove excess slurry with a finger of the right hand, while supporting the outside of the pedestal wall with the left hand. Remove the pot from the wheel and allow to slowly dry upside down until the join has set. The join will be very strong once the pot is fired, but is a point of weakness until this happens, so do be careful with it.

Turning surface decorations

When we consider surface decoration on pots we usually think of the colored, glazed surface. However, decoration added to a thrown or turned surface ultimately affects the finished look of a pot and can create interest and individualism in our pottery. Surface marks can be created using the fingers or tools on soft, newly thrown or leather-hard pots. Here are a few different ideas to inspire you, but look around you to find everyday objects that can be used to create more unusual and interesting surfaces. The type of clay used will affect the

Thrown surfaces

When the clay is freshly thrown it is very soft so can be easily marked by fingers or tools. Often the best way to create a surface decoration is to use a throwing rib to smooth the surface flat first, then add the texture so that throwing rings do not interrupt the design.

finely grooved
To create a finely grooved surface, use a serrated kidney. First smooth the surface of the pot with a throwing rib by supporting the pot on the inside with your left hand and pushing it against the rib on the outside. With both hands on the outside of the pot, place the kidney on the surface of the clay wall as the wheel rotates slowly. Hold it very still to create smooth even lines around the pot. This decoration can be used all over the pot or just on one area to add a detail. It can make a pot look very industrial.

different shaped ridges
To create a variety of different shaped ridges, cut a series of grooves into an old phone or credit card to make a "former." Metal formers also can be bought from pottery suppliers. They will last longer but you have no control over the design. You do not need to smooth the surface with a throwing rib first. A fair amount of pressure needs to be exerted on the former to push the design onto the surface of the pot, so support the pot on the inside with the fingers of the left hand as the right hand pushes the former onto the surface on the outside. Formers like this can be used to create foot rings or interesting lips to pots, as well as an allover surface decoration.

using the roulette
This texture is made using a homemade roulette. First, smooth the surface of the pot with a throwing rib by supporting the pot on the inside with your left hand and pushing it against the rib on the outside. Place an old hollow cog over a hole-making tool and hold this against the surface of the revolving pot. The cog rotates as the pot does, creating this interesting surface texture. Many variations of this tool can be tried, such as a roulette made from plaster or lino, or they can be purchased ready to use on rollers with a handle. Traditionally, some potteries had the name of their pottery cut into a roulette that was imprinted onto the surface of the pot.

final result. Clay with a lot of grit or grog in it will create a much rougher surface than fine, smooth clay. Obviously more than one technique can be used on a pot to create variations in finish.

spiral grooves

You can use the first finger of the right hand to push a groove into the surface of the pot. Support the pot on the inside with the fingers of the left hand, then push the finger gently onto the surface of the wet pot and slowly draw up the pot to create a continuous spiraling groove. This groove is similar to the ones created during throwing if a rib is not used to smooth the surface. More or less pressure can be applied to create different depths of groove, though the deeper the groove the more difficult it is to get it to spiral neatly up the pot without distorting the whole shape.

deep grooves

The first finger of the right hand can push very deep grooves into the surface of the pot. Here they are evenly spaced and do not spiral up the pot. Various shapes and sizes of grooves can be created in this way, but the surface of the pot may need to be lubricated with a little water to stop the finger dragging on the surface and distorting the shape. This design has the effect of narrowing the appearance of the cylinder. The fingers of the left hand support the clay wall on the inside to prevent the pot from wobbling.

ridges

These ridges are created using a throwing action. Support the clay on the inside with the left hand, then thin the spaces between the ridges in the normal way, leaving the thick ridges behind. Ridges like this can be placed at any interval and in as many numbers as you require. They can be defined a little more by being squeezed between the fingers and thumb of the right hand to make them sharper.

Turned surfaces

Adding texture to leather-hard pots, firm to the touch but still damp, invariably involves the use of tools to cut the surface, as the fingers make little impression at this stage. Unlike wet surface decoration, clay is removed from the pot during these processes. For these techniques the leather-hard or softer pot is first recentered on the wheel head after it has been allowed to dry a little (see pages 114–117).

smooth grooves

Ribbon tools are found in a variety of shapes and sizes and can be used to create many turned surfaces. They are ideal for creating turned grooves as they cut neatly into the pot, removing unwanted clay. They are already shaped into curves, so it is only a matter of holding them steady against the wall of the pot. The amount of pressure and the amount of time spent will determine the depth of each groove. To create smooth, concave grooves such as these, the clay needs to be slightly softer than leather hard. Hold the tool in the right hand and use the left hand to support the wall of the pot and add extra pressure to the tool to help hold it still against the pot. The wheel should be rotating fairly swiftly to make turning much easier and more precise.

deep grooves

A clean and precisely cut design, as if it were machine turned, needs to be turned on a pot that is a bit dryer than leather hard. Use a very sharp triangular turning tool to cut the deep, sharp grooves into the surface of the pot. Hold the tool in the right hand and use the left hand to support the wall of the pot on the inside and add extra pressure to the tool to help hold it steady. The wheel should be rotating fairly swiftly to make turning much easier and more precise. Take great care with sharp tools so that you do not injure yourself or cut the pot too deeply. A design like this could be cut all over the pot or restricted to one place to create a feature.

light, wavy grooves

To create a lightly grooved wavy line, use a serrated kidney. If the kidney is held in position against the wall of the pot it will, eventually, cut a regular series of grooves into the surface, but here we only want to create a light surface decoration. Let the wheel rotate fairly slowly and place the kidney on the surface with the left hand supporting the pot on the inside and the left thumb adding extra pressure to the tool to help hold it still. Quickly move the kidney up and down to create a wavy line. Remove the tool from the surface after one revolution of the wheel, otherwise the pattern will distort if worked over again. This technique creates a lot of burrs on the surface, but leave the pot to dry and these will easily brush off later.

random grooves

Not all turned surface decorations have to be precise and controlled. Here, the corner of a ribbon tool is used to create a series of random grooves. Place the tool on the surface of the pot with the left hand supporting from the inside. As the wheel slowly rotates, move the tool up and down the surface to create a continuous groove that has no regular pattern. You can experiment with different tools and wheel speeds to create variations on this theme. Also, two grooves could be made some distance apart and then filled in with a random groove pattern to produce a band of decoration rather than an allover texture; it would look more controlled and less messy.

fluting

Not all surface decoration has to go horizontally around a pot. To create a fluted surface, first measure the circumference of the pot and divide it into equally spaced segments. Very carefully use a sharp ribbon tool to cut vertically between the guidelines to remove clay and create the flutes. Support the pot on the outside with the left hand. Do not try to remove all the clay at once, but shave it away gradually, keeping within the guidelines.

This is a very slow process and requires patience. You can choose to flute the full length of the pot or just work on one area or band. The spacing of the grooves can also be varied. Be careful not to make the flutes too deep as they may thin the wall too much. You may find it easier to hold the pot in your hand rather than on the wheel, and pull the tool toward you rather than upward.

faceting

This surface decoration is known as "faceting." The pot needs to be quite thick as a lot of clay is removed to create this finish. The pot should also be a little softer than leather hard to make cutting easier. Measure the circumference of the pot and divide it into equal segments, usually fairly wide. Use a potato peeler or a kidney to shave away the clay between the guidelines, removing the curve to leave a flat surface. Support the pot on the outside with the left hand. You may find it easier to hold the pot in the left hand rather than on the wheel and draw the tool toward you.

Lids, Handles & Knobs

The three elements of lid, handle, and knob can be used to express individualism in your pottery. The range and variety of these additions is infinite. In this chapter various wheel forming techniques and designs are explored to show how they can be created. This is, however, in no way a complete compendium of every possibility.

As your confidence on the wheel grows, more complex variations can be achieved and new ideas explored. Many potters develop styles of knobs, for example, that are instantly recognized across their work. Such details can tie a collection of objects together under one uniting theme.

Making these items should be fun and exciting, creating new possibilities and exploring new avenues.

Rim-resting lids

Lids that rest on the rim of a pot are simple to create. They have no galleries to sit into, so accuracy in fit is not absolutely vital. These lids have no knobs as they could be easily picked up without—but knobs can be added later (see pages 154–157).

Flat lid with flange

A lid like this is best suited to narrow pot forms because it is very flat. If it were very wide it could slump in the middle or warp during firing. A simple storage jar like this could be made in a variety of sizes. This type of jar is not typical of kitchenware, but would be more suited to the dressing table.

Measure the outside width of the pot using a pair of calipers. Leave the calipers set to this width and put to one side until the lid has been formed and you need to check its size.

2 Center the clay on the wheel head (see pages 20–21) and form it into a flat disk shape by pressing down on top with the right hand. The left hand is steadying the right during this process. Lubricate the hands and clay with water as needed.

3 Open out the flat disk of clay using the fingers of the left hand in the center, while the right hand helps to hold the left steady as this process proceeds. Draw a wall of clay outward with the left fingers, leaving a flat, level base.

4 Push the wall of clay inward a little, using the thumb of the left hand on the outside while the fingers remain on the inside. Leave a ledge of clay the same thickness as the base. Use the side of the right hand to smooth the rim of the wall as it is formed. Use the little finger of the right hand pressed against the flange to define the wall.

5 Check the outside width of the lid using the preset calipers. Wire the lid and leave to dry a little. When it is leather hard, position it upside down centrally on the wheel head (see pages 114–117). Use a ribbon tool to gently smooth the surface. Rest the left hand on the lid, with the left thumb against the tool to hold it steady. The wheel should be traveling fairly swiftly.

6 If the lid is still slightly too big, use the ribbon tool to trim clay from the width.

Use the fingers to define the flange after it has been formed.

Both hands touch one another to give added stability during throwing.

The lid base and walls are of even thickness.

The flange hangs down into the pot to prevent it from being easily knocked off.

The lid top is completely flat.

The lid slightly overlaps the pot. This looks better than if it was exactly the right size or too small. It also makes it easier to grip when in use.

The pot walls and lid are of an even thickness.

Outside fitting cap lid

The lid on this ginger jar rests on the rim of the pot and the lid rim rests on the pot walls. This lid is simple to create, as it is basically a small inverted bowl. Although a good fit is important, it does not matter if it is a little big, as it is unlikely to be easily knocked off.

Repeat step 1 on page 138. Center the clay on the wheel head (see pages 20–21). Push the right-hand thumb into the center of the clay and open it out. Use the left hand to support the clay wall on the outside as it is pushed out. Lubricate the hands and clay with water as needed.

1

Place the left thumb at the outside base of the lid and the left fingers inside. Your right hand rests on top of the left to provide support. Squeeze the fingers and thumb to thin the clay. Pull the left hand up the wall to further raise the walls. Further thinning can be done with fingers. Use the side of the right hand to smooth the rim.

2

Smooth the outside wall of the small pot using a throwing rib. Push the wall gently onto the rib with the left fingers on the inside of the pot. Hold the flat edge of the rib on the wheel head and push it slightly under the base of the pot, giving a bevel finish.

3

Measure the inside width of the lid using the preset calipers to make sure it will fit over the neck of the jar. Measure the depth of the lid to make sure it will rest on the outside of the jar. Wire the lid and slide it off the wheel onto the right hand. Put to one side to dry a little.

4

When the lid is leather hard, reposition it upside down and centrally on the wheel head (see pages 114–117). Using a ribbon tool, remove any imperfections by gently shaving away clay. Hold the tool in the right hand and rest the left hand on the lid, with the left thumb against the tool to hold it steady. The wheel should be traveling fairly swiftly.

5

Form the lid's smooth, curved corners by removing the sharp edges with the ribbon tool.

6

The fingers smooth and raise a small wall.

The base is flat and even.

The curved edges of the lid soften the form to correspond with the curved body of the jar.

The cap lid sits neatly over the rim of the jar.

The rim of the lid sits on top of the shoulder of the pot.

The wall and base of the lid are of an even thickness.

Domed lid with flange

This lid rests on the rim of the pot, while the flange holds it in place. The lid rim hangs over the pot walls as a decorative feature that could be exaggerated to create a different finish. The domed lid follows the profile of the curved pot and so is in harmony with the form as a whole.

Measure the inside width of the rim of the pot using a pair of calipers. Leave the calipers set to this width and put to one side. You will need them once the lid has been formed to check its size.

Center the clay on the wheel head (see pages 20–21). Push the right-hand thumb into the center of the clay and open it out. Push a small wall of clay outward to widen the hole, supporting the wall with the left hand on the outside. Lubricate the clay with water when necessary.

1

2

3 **4** **5** **6** **7**

3 Use the fingers of the left hand to form the curved inside base of the lid. Place the thumb of the left hand at the outside base of the pot and the left fingers inside. Place your right hand on top of the clay wall and the left hand to provide support. Squeeze the left fingers and thumb to draw up a thick wall of clay.

4 Form the thick wall into a wall and ledge by pressing down, using the little finger of the right hand on the outside of the wall. Support the rim as you do this with the left hand.

5 Check the width of the flange using the preset calipers to make sure it will drop into the pot. If the flange is too wide, push it in a little with the little finger of the right hand. If it is too narrow, pull it out a little. Wire the lid, keeping the wire taut and completely flat with the wheel head and pulling it toward you. Place to one side to dry a little.

6 When the lid is leather hard, center it upside down on the wheel head (see pages 114–117). Use a ribbon tool to begin turning away the excess clay. Hold the tool in the right hand and rest the left hand on the pot, with the left thumb against the tool to hold it steady. The wheel should be traveling fairly swiftly.

7 Use the ribbon tool to trim the rim of the lid so it follows the inside shape. Form the top into a neat dome and turn the rim into a ledge, so that it replicates the shape underneath, by trimming the clay away from the width of the top of the lid. Use a ribbon tool to remove the excess clay that has supported the wide lid during throwing.

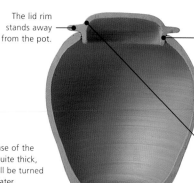

The fingers define the shape of the wall and ledge.

The ledge is formed from the thickness of the walls.

The lid rim stands away from the pot.

The flange hangs down into the pot.

The lid and pot walls are of an even thickness.

The lid is slightly domed.

The base of the lid is quite thick, this will be turned away later.

Recessed lid

This unusual lid hangs down into the pot. The lid itself could be used to hold paperclips or other small items. With a knob added, lids like this are used on some casserole dishes.

Measure the outside width of the pot using a pair of calipers. Leave the calipers set to this width and put to one side until the lid has been formed and you need to check its size.

Center the clay on the wheel head (see pages 20–21). Push the right-hand thumb into the center of the clay and open it out. Use the left hand to support the clay wall on the outside as it is pushed out and to help keep the right hand steady. Lubricate the clay and hands when needed.

3
Place the thumb of the left hand at the outside base and the left fingers inside. Place the right hand on top of the clay wall and the left hand to provide support. Squeeze the fingers and thumb to thin the clay. Ease this hand up to further raise the wall. Draw the wall outward to form a small bowl with a thick rim.

4
Squeeze the left thumb and fingers together again to pull the rim of the bowl outward horizontally to form a lip. Use the little finger of the right hand to smooth the rim flat.

5
Check the width of the lid using the preset calipers. It should be the same or just marginally larger. If the lid is too small, squeeze the clay out a little more, until the right width is achieved. Wire the lid from the wheel by keeping the wire taut and completely flat with the wheel head and pulling it toward you. Place the lid to one side to dry a little.

6
When the lid is leather hard, center it upside down on the wheel head (see pages 114–117). Begin to trim away excess clay from under the rim using a ribbon tool. Hold the tool in the right hand and rest the left hand on the pot, with the left thumb against the tool to hold it steady. The wheel should be traveling fairly swiftly.

7
Use the ribbon tool to trim the lid in the middle to follow the shape of the bowl inside. The rim should be wide enough to sit on the rim of the pot, while the bowl hangs down inside.

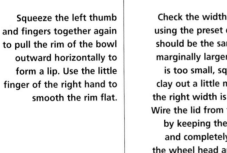

The fingers of the left hand draw out the clay wall, creating a small bowl form.

The little finger of the right hand smooths the rim of the pot.

The walls of the lid and pot are of a similar thickness.

Excess clay is left under the rim to support it during throwing. This will be turned away later.

The rim of the lid sits on the rim of the pot.

The bowl hangs down to hold the lid in place.

Lids on galleries

These lids are more complicated to make because the measuring of the gallery and lid has to be done much more accurately. These lids usually have knobs to lift them out of their recessed galleries. The tighter fit makes them more suited to the storage of dry foods in the kitchen.

Flat lid

This very simple, quick lid requires no turning. Because it sits flat it can look rather plain, but various different knobs could be formed to add interest. Functional and easy to clean, this lid makes an ideal storage vessel for the kitchen.

Measure the inside width of the gallery of the pot using a pair of calipers. Leave the calipers set to this width and put to one side until the lid has been formed and you need to check its size.

Center the clay on the wheel (see pages 20–21) and begin to shape the lid. Flatten the clay away from the center with the side of the right hand, leaving a knob of clay in the middle. Support the outside wall with the left hand and lubricate with water whenever it begins to dry out.

3 Use the fingers of the right hand to form the clay left in the middle into roughly the shape of the knob you want (see pages 154–157). Smooth the width of the lid using the fingers of the left hand.

4 Supporting the knob with the left hand, define the shape with the right. Use the little finger of the right hand to push a slight bevel at the base of the knob. This allows the fingers a better grip to remove the lid when in use.

5 Use the preset calipers to check the width of the lid. If it is too big, trim the width with a turning tool. If it is too small, flatten the clay out a little more to increase the diameter, making sure not to make it too thin. Create a bevel under the base using the throwing rib to remove a sliver of clay. This will make it easier to remove the lid from the wheel.

6 As this lid is wide and thin, it will not lift off easily. Flood the wheel head with water and wire the lid, keeping the wire taut and completely flat with the wheel head and pulling it toward you. Push the lid across the wheel with the left hand onto the fingers of the right hand. Put aside to dry a little.

7 Before the lid is completely dry, use a sponge to smooth its base. This lid is now finished and does not require turning.

The fingers form the knob of the lid.

The little finger undercuts the knob to make it easier to pick up.

The clay is flattened to form a flat lid.

The lid is flush with the rim of the pot.

The knob makes the lid easy to remove.

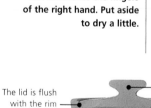

The lid sits neatly on the gallery.

Domed lid

Domed lids like this are the most common forms found in kitchens. The lids are easy to remove and the whole shape is very functional. This lid can be successfully made much larger and wider to cover a casserole dish because its domed shape means it will not sag or distort during firing.

Measure the width of the gallery of the pot using a pair of calipers. Leave the calipers set to this width and put to one side until the lid has been formed and you need to check its size.

Center the clay (see pages 20–21) into a tall, narrow cylinder. Push the thumb of the right hand halfway down into the center of the revolving clay. Support the wall on the outside with the left hand, especially since such a narrow pot could be prone to wobbling.

1

2

3

4

5

6

7

3 Place the thumb of the left hand at the base of the outside of the pot and the left fingers on the inside. Place your right hand on top of the clay wall and the left hand. Squeeze the clay between the fingers and thumb to open the clay out to form a small bowl. Lubricate the hands with water as needed.

4 Smooth the edge of the small bowl flat with the side of the right hand or little finger. This area needs to be flat to sit on the gallery of the pot.

5 Check the width of the lid with the preset calipers. Wire the lid from the wheel, and allow it to dry a little. Once the rim has stiffened, turn it upside down to dry the thick base. When the lid is leather hard, place it centrally upside down on the wheel (see pages 114–117).

6 Form the knob by removing slivers of clay wth a ribbon tool, held in the right hand. Rest the left hand on the pot, with the thumb against the tool to hold it steady. The wheel should be traveling fairly swiftly. Use the ribbon tool to dome the lid to correlate to the bowl form inside.

7 Continue to remove small ribbons of clay until the desired shape is created. When turning is finished, gently push the lid away from you, across the wheel, to loosen the suction. Then lift the lid off the wheel. Remove the lid from the wheel and leave to dry. Before it is completely dry, use a hole-making tool to hollow out the knob from inside.

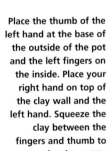

The little finger of the right hand smooths and flattens the rim.

The fingers of the left hand form the shape of the bowl.

The base is very thick. A knob will be turned out of this later.

The knob is quite thick so it has been hollowed out from underneath to aid with even drying.

The lid is domed and stands proud of the pot.

The flat rim of the lid sits neatly in the gallery.

Domed lid with flange

The deep flange holds the lid firmly in place and gives a tight seal. The curve of the lid follows the curve of the pot so they work well together as a whole form. Any variety of knob could be turned for this lid to add your own individual touch. This classic storage jar could be used to store dry ingredients such as pasta or rice.

Measure the inside width of the gallery using a pair of calipers. Leave the calipers set to this width and put to one side. You will need them once the lid has been formed to check its size.

Center the clay (see pages 20–21) and form it into a narrow cylinder. Use the thumb of the right hand to open out the clay. Push it only halfway down the cylinder and support the outside wall with the left hand.

1

2

3

4

5

6

7

3 Use the right thumb to open out the clay into a thick wall. Support the widening clay with the left hand from underneath.

4 Place the left-hand thumb at the outside base and the left fingers on the inside. Rest the right hand on top of the clay wall and the left hand. Squeeze the clay between the fingers and thumb to thin it. Use the left hand to push the top part of the wall back in on itself to form a flange and ledge. Lubricate the clay so you do not snag the delicate clay walls of this lid.

5 Check the width of the lid with the preset calipers. Make sure the flange width is narrower than the opening in the pot so it will drop inside. Wire the lid from the wheel, and put it aside to dry a little. When the flange has stiffened, turn the lid over so the thick base that will form the knob can dry.

6 When the lid is leather hard, it is ready to turn. Center the lid upside down on the wheel (see pages 114–117). Begin to remove the excess clay carefully with a ribbon tool. Hold the tool in the right hand and rest the left hand on the pot, with the left thumb against the tool to hold it steady. The wheel should be traveling fairly swiftly.

7 Use the ribbon tool to form the dome of the lid to correspond to the bowl form inside, and create the shape of the knob (see pages 154–157). Avoid removing too much clay accidentally. Carefully remove the lid from the wheel. Before it is completely dry, use a hole-making tool to hollow out the knob from the inside.

The inside shape of the lid is bowl-like.

The right-hand little finger defines the shape of the ledge.

The left fingers and thumb create the flange by pushing the wall of clay inward.

The thick base will be used to form the knob.

The flange hangs down into the pot to secure the lid in place.

The ledge of the lid sits neatly on the gallery.

The knob has been hollowed out from underneath to aid with even drying.

The lid and pot walls are of an even thickness.

Drop-in lid

The advantages of a drop-in lid like this is that nothing stands proud of the rim, so knobs are not accidentally caught or knocked off. It is also possible to stack one storage jar on top of another. The bowl of the lid containing the knob acts as a flange, holding the lid in place. Lids like this are commonly used on casserole dishes because the knob does not get caught on the shelves of the oven.

Measure the inside width of the gallery using a pair of calipers. Leave the calipers set to this width and put to one side until the lid has been formed and you need to check its size.

Center the clay (see pages 20–21) and flatten it using the side of the right hand, working away from the center of the revolving clay. Support the wall on the outside with the left hand. A knob of clay will be left in the center. Lubricate the fingers and clay with water as needed.

3 Place the thumb of the left hand at the base of the outside of the lid and the left fingers on the inside. Place your right hand on top of the left hand to provide support. Squeeze the clay between the fingers and thumb of the left hand to form a thick wall.

4 The shape of the knob needs to be finished before the wall is completed. Use the right hand to shape the bulge in the center of the lid into a knob. Do not make this knob too tall. It needs to remain below the height of the outside walls. Push under the knob with the little finger of the right hand to undercut it so it will be easy to grip.

5 Squeeze the lip of the lid between the left thumb and fingers to raise the wall above the height of the knob (to make turning possible), and flatten it to form a wide rim. Smooth the rim using the first finger of the right hand. Check the width with the preset calipers, and wire it from the wheel. When the lid is leather hard, center it upside down on the wheel.

6 Use a ribbon tool to turn away the excess clay. Hold the tool in the right hand and rest the left hand on the pot, with the left thumb against the tool to steady it. The wheel should be traveling fairly swiftly; turning is much easier if the wheel moves quickly because less pressure is required to remove slivers of clay.

7 Continue removing clay with the ribbon tool until the lid looks like a little hat with a domed center and rim that is wide enough to sit on the gallery of the pot, so the dome hangs down inside. Carefully remove the lid from the wheel. Before it is completely dry, use a hole-making tool to hollow out the knob from inside.

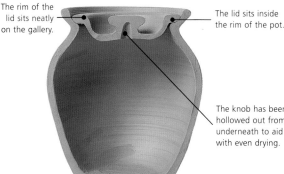

The knob has an undercut to make it easy to grip.

The little finger of the right hand smooths the rim of the lid.

The fingers and thumb of the left hand form the wall.

The wall is higher than the knob.

The rim of the lid sits neatly on the gallery.

The lid sits inside the rim of the pot.

The knob has been hollowed out from underneath to aid with even drying.

Sealed pot lids

The advantage of these techniques is that no separate lid needs to be made, so there is no need to measure anything. However, to make a sealed form takes a great deal of practice.

Simple cutaway lid

This is a very decorative lidded pot and is more suited to the dressing table than the kitchen. It could hold cotton or large pieces of jewelry, but is not suitable for storing foodstuffs.

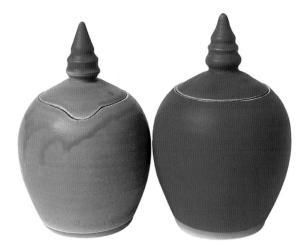

1 Throw a pot that is collared in and sealed at the top. When this pot has dried to slightly softer than leather hard, firm to the touch but still damp, the lid can be created. Re-attach the pot to the wheel head by dampening it slightly. Using a pin attached to a stick, slowly cut through the surface of the pot. The wheel should be revolving slowly and the hands held very steady. The lid can be cut out at any point near the top of the pot.

2 Continue to cut through the wall of the pot at a downward angle. Support the pot with the left hand as it rotates.

3 When the pin has cut right through the thickness of the wall, lift the lid away from the pot. The lid will fit perfectly and the curve of the pot will not be interrupted. Carefully trim away any burrs of clay that have been created with a knife. Be careful not to alter the shape of the lid.

4 Alternatively, a locating lug can be cut into the pot while the lid is being cut with the pin on a stick. This process requires a steady hand because you cannot rotate the wheel to get a perfect circle. You might like to first mark a faint guideline to assist you.

The lid is cut at an angle so it has some grip on the base.

The lid fits perfectly onto the pot and the join is practically invisible.

Cutaway lid with flange

This style of lid and flange could be created on any number of shaped, sealed pots. This particular pot would be suitable as a trinket box rather than a storage vessel for the kitchen. Its delicate form could hold treasured possessions such as jewelry. As with any sealed pot, the lid could be cut off at any number of points on the body to make the opening smaller or larger.

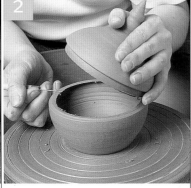

1	2	3	4
Throw a pot that is collared in and sealed at the top. Using a piece of an old credit or phone card, push a groove into the surface of the wet pot around the center, pushing in past the thickness of the pot walls. When the pot is leather hard, use a pin on a stick to cut through the wall at the base of the groove.	Rotate the wheel slowly and place the left hand on the top of the pot to prevent the lid flying off. Slowly push the pin horizontally into the base of the groove as the wheel rotates. The lid will eventually be cut free from the base. Do this very slowly so as not to break the lid. You now have a lid with a flange and a base pot.	Clean up the base a little to remove burrs of clay that may have formed during the cutting process. Slowly spin the wheel and gently smooth the edges using a ribbon tool. Also use the ribbon tool to remove a little clay from the inside of the rim to ensure a good fit.	Clean away any bits of clay from the flange of the lid with a knife so that it drops neatly into the base. If it does not, trim a little more clay away from the inside rim of the base with a ribbon tool. Do this very slowly and gradually so as not to break the delicate rim.

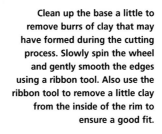

The flange hangs down inside the pot to hold it in place.

The lid sits on the rim of the base neatly.

The outside of the pot is an uninterrupted curve.

Handles

Handles for pots can be made in many different ways. Shown here are the most popular and frequently used methods. Handles allow you to impart your own style on a pot, so be prepared to experiment and find your favorite.

Wire-extruded handle

Wire-extruded handles are easy to make. This one is also very cheap because the wire that seals bags of clay is formed into a handle-shaped loop. Different shaped and more durable handle loops can be purchased from pottery suppliers.

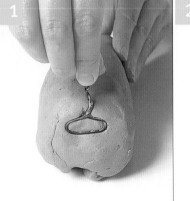

1 Form the clay into a fat sausage and position a wire loop tool at one end, below the surface of the sausage.

2 Draw the loop tool smoothly and swiftly through the sausage of clay, trying to keep the tool at the same height to avoid lumps in the handle. Drag the tool right through to the other side of the sausage, keeping it in an upright position. Carefully peel back the clay to reveal the handle within.

3 Carefully remove the handle and leave to stiffen a little before attaching it to the pot. This method can be used to make both large and small handles, though longer handles would require a larger sausage of clay and it may be more difficult to draw the tool through evenly for a long length.

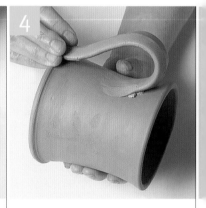

4 The handle should have stiffened a little so it is not floppy, but not so stiff that when it is bent into a curve it splits. Use a craft knife to crosshatch the area of the pot that one end of the handle will be attached to, and dab on a little slurry. Fix the handle end to this area and smooth the join into the pot with your fingers. Curve the handle into a loop, judging the loop by eye and ensuring it is practical as well as graceful. Fix the other end of the handle to the pot and smooth the join as before.

Extruded handle

Extruded handles have a good deal of strength because the clay is compressed through a precut die. The choice of dies is infinite, and you can make your own. An extruder or "wad box" is needed to push the clay through the die. This method is reasonably expensive because the equipment needs to be purchased.

1 All manner of shapes can be created using different dies in the extruder, and not all of these are used as handles. They can be used to add decorative features all over the pot as ridges or to create feet, knobs, or handles. If you go to the expense of purchasing an extruder you will soon find new ways to use it. Precut dies for circles and squares can be purchased with the extruder. Blank dies can also be bought to create your own shapes.

2 Fill the body of the hollow extruder with clay and pull the handle down to force the clay through the die. The advantage of this method is that identical handles can be made easily and at speed. Longer handles can also be easily formed. Long lengths are extruded and then cut into shorter pieces. You can place the extruded shape on a board to dry a little, but because the clay has been compressed it is strong and will hold its shape readily. Short handles can be placed in a curve to dry a little, thus preventing them from cracking when they are formed into a loop.

3 Use a craft knife to crosshatch the area of the pot that one end of the handle will be attached to and dab on a little slurry. Fix one end of the handle to this area and smooth the join into the pot with your fingers. Curve the handle into a loop, judging the loop by eye and ensuring it is practical as well as graceful. Fix the other end of the handle to the pot and smooth the join as before. Using a turntable allows you to move the pot around easily and study the profile of the handle before deciding on its final position.

4 Here a long handle has been extruded and left to stiffen in its final curve before being attached. Because it is such a long handle it could easily go out of shape when attached in such a wide loop.

Pulled and joined handles

There are two ways to pull handles. One is to make the handle separately, the other is to attach the clay to the pot and then pull it. Pulling handles separately is the easier technique. It takes as much practice to pull a handle as it does to learn to throw, so do not be disheartened if your first attempts are unsuccessful. It is a very difficult technique to describe, and if you can get someone to show you how to do it, all the better.

1 Form the clay into a fat sausage and hold it in the left hand. Lubricate the hand and clay with water and stroke the clay with the right hand to smooth it.

2 Place the thumb of the right hand across the front of the sausage of clay, and the fingers around the back to create a crook. Gently run the hand down the full length of the sausage. You are stroking and gently easing the clay downward to lengthen and thin it. Make sure the hands and clay are wet; if the clay snags on the fingers it may tear the strap prematurely from the sausage. After a few strokes, rotate the clay so that the profile is kept and your fingers do not flatten one area more than another. The handle section should be elliptical in shape. All handmade handles tend to be this shape because it is a stronger, more comfortable shape to hold than a round section.

3 As the handle gets longer, use the thumb to form two grooves on either side of it, creating a raised ridge in the middle as a decorative feature. This is not absolutely necessary, a flat profile is also fine, or you could create your own design. Keep stroking and lengthening the clay until the required size is achieved. This is a mug handle, so only the bottom few inches of the strap will be used.

4 Either place the handle or handles flat on a board or along the edge of a table. You can rest the strap of clay on the edge of the table and, above this, push it down onto the tabletop to hold it in place. This creates a slight curve in the top of the handle and allows the air to circulate around it, speeding up the stiffening process. Be careful they do not dry too much before you use them.

5 Use a craft knife to crosshatch the area of the pot that the top end of the handle will be attached to and dab on a little slurry. Cut the handle from the table (or lift it from a board) and press the thickest end onto the prepared area. Smooth the join into the pot with your fingers. Curve the handle into a loop, judging the loop by eye and ensuring it is practical as well as graceful. Fix the other end of the handle to the pot and smooth the join as before.

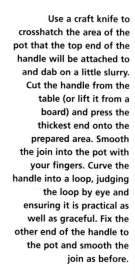

Handle pulled directly on the pot

This is a very difficult process and should only be attempted when you are practiced and confident about pulling handles. For many pots this method creates the best kind of handle because it is a part of the organic whole and the handle springs from the pot in a very natural way.

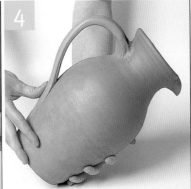

1 Use a craft knife to crosshatch the area of the pot that one end of the handle will be attached to and dab on a little slurry. Attach a sausage of clay to the crosshatched area and smooth the clay all around the join to seal the joint and ensure a strong hold.

2 Support the pot in the left hand and pull the handle with the right. Keep the handle hanging straight down so as not to put any unnecessary stress on it. Lubricate the handle and right hand with water. Hold the handle between the thumb and fingers of the right hand and begin to pull it. Gently stroke the clay downward, thinning and lengthening the handle. Do this very gradually and slowly. Tugging on the clay may pull it off the pot or cause an area of weakness by thinning the clay too much in one place. The handle should taper slightly from top to bottom. Let gravity help the lengthening process.

3 This handle has two decorative grooves in it formed by running the thumb down the length of the handle on alternate sides, keeping the fingers crooked around the back of the handle to press the clay against and to hold the thumb steady as it travels down the length of the handle. Remember to keep the hands well lubricated and the handle vertical at all times.

4 Curve the handle and assess the position before attaching it permanently to the other end, as before. A smooth flowing curve that springs from the pot naturally is what you are trying to achieve, and standing back from the pot will help you see the form as a whole. A small coil of clay can be added to the join and smoothed with the fingers to help strengthen it.

Thrown handles

Handles can be made by using thrown sections cut to shape or by throwing whole handle forms. Handles that are thrown are rounded.

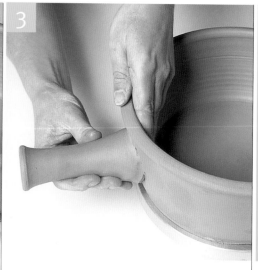

1

Here a matching pair of knob handles, small pots with no bases, have been thrown. Use a craft knife to crosshatch the base of each handle and an area on the side of the pot and dab on a little slurry. Push the first handle firmly into position over the crosshatching and use your fingers to smooth the join. Attach the second handle in the same way, ensuring they are placed directly opposite one another. When this pot is fired the handles will be very strong, but until then they remain very fragile so do not use them to move the pot and be careful not to knock them off.

2

A single handle has been thrown here. It is hollow and has been shaped so it is easy to grip, being wider at both ends and narrower in the middle. As the pot wall has a slight angle to it, the base of the handle is cut at an angle. When it is fixed in position it will stick straight out from the pot, otherwise it would point downward and look odd.

3

Use a craft knife to crosshatch the handle and the pot, and dab slurry onto the pot. Press the handle firmly into place over the crosshatching and smooth the join with the fingers. You could also attach and smooth a coil of clay around the join to strengthen it. Again, this handle is weak in its raw state and would not support the weight of the pot, but when it is fired, as long as the join is good, it will be very strong.

Lugs

Lug handles are attached to the sides of urns or casserole dishes. They are placed on opposite sides of a heavy pot so it can be lifted with both hands. They are placed horizontally on the pot, rather than vertically like mug handles.

method 1

Throw a short cylinder of clay (see pages 24–27), with no base, that is narrower at the rim than the base. Keep the base and rim slightly heavy to create a strong profile. When the clay is just softer than leather hard, use a craft knife to cut the wall of the cylinder in half at an angle so the finished lug becomes narrower at the outside. Cut a "V"-shaped piece of clay from the wall of the cylinder on both sides, leaving two identical lugs. Use the craft knife to crosshatch the edges of the lug and the parts where the handles are to be attached.

Dab some slurry onto the crosshatched areas of the pot and push the lugs firmly onto the pot, supporting the pot from inside with the left hand to prevent distorting its shape. Use the fingers to smooth the join and remove any excess slurry that has squeezed out of the join, both on top of the lug and underneath. Smooth any sharp corners on the lugs with a sponge.

method 2

A strap handle, either pulled or extruded (see pages 148–151) could be used as a lug. Smooth the ends of the handle onto the pot and let the width of the handle stand at right angles to the wall. Make sure the section of handle you use is wide enough for the fingers to fit under when the pot is in use because a good grip is essential on a full pot of stew. Handles made in this way are softer than the pot, so dry the whole thing slowly under plastic to equalize the moisture content and stop the lug cracking.

Lubricate the clay and hands with water and squeeze the clay between the thumb on the top of the lug and the fingers underneath, using a back and forth movement along the length of the sausage. Make the clay thinner at the point it is farthest away from the pot, creating a lug that is pleasant to hold and well attached. Do not overthin. Lugs should be on the heavier side. This is a traditional method of making lugs for utility and domestic pots.

Turned knobs

A lid thrown upside down can be left with a very thick pedestal base from which to turn a decorative knob.

Center the lid upside down on the wheel head (see pages 114–117). Use a ribbon tool to remove clay quickly from the sides of the lid. Hold the tool in the right hand and rest the left hand on the lid, with the left thumb against the tool to hold it steady. The wheel should be traveling fairly swiftly.

Continue removing clay until a general knob shape is created (see below). When you are happy with your knob, carefully remove the lid from the wheel and leave to dry. Before it is completely dry, use a hole-making tool to hollow out the knob from the inside.

rounded ball knob
To create this rounded ball knob, use a rounded ribbon tool to slowly remove clay from the revolving knob. This style of knob could be used on a variety of storage jars and trinket boxes.

simple knob
Use a flat ribbon tool to form the flat surface of this simple knob. Cut clay away from underneath the knob to make it easy to grip. This knob is ideal for kitchen storage vessels.

decorative knob
A variety of different-shaped ribbon tools can be used to create a highly decorative knob. Such a high degree of decoration needs to be carried out very slowly, so as not to remove the wrong bits of clay. A knob like this could be used on trinket boxes.

hollow knob
This knob is hollowed out of the lid. Use a ribbon tool to carefully remove clay from inside the knob as the wheel rotates. You may have to stop the wheel and clean out turnings from the hole to see what you are doing. This knob is suitable for a casserole dish, as it is large enough to grip while wearing oven gloves.

The knob is hollowed out from underneath to aid with even drying.

The knob is rounded but not spherical, otherwise it may have looked too big.

A simple design can look elegant and understated.

This knob is easy to grip even with wet hands.

The concentric rings on this knob decrease proportionally, giving a pleasing effect.

More clay could have been used during throwing to allow the potter to make a taller knob.

The knob is hollowed out from above and the inside curve echoes the outside.

The knob and lid walls are of an even thickness.

Knobs thrown separately and joined

Throwing knobs separately means you do not have to throw lids with thick pedestals or risk destroying your lid during turning. However, small amounts of clay can be difficult to throw.

Center the clay on the wheel head (see pages 20–21). Use the fingers of both hands to shape a simple, solid knob (see below). Press the little finger into the base of the knob to form an undercut. Then wire the knob from the wheel. Put the knob aside until it is on the soft side of leather hard. Center a leather-hard lid on the wheel (see pages 114–117).

Use a craft knife to crosshatch an area in the center of the lid. Add a little slurry to the crosshatched area to act as a glue. Push the knob onto the crosshatched area. Rotate the wheel to check that the knob is positioned centrally. Use the little finger of the right hand to smooth the join. Remove the lid from the wheel and leave to dry. Before it is completely dry, use a hole-making tool to hollow out the knob from the inside.

decorative knob
This decorative knob is made from a tall, centered piece of clay. Using the fingers, push concentric rings into the cylindrical knob.

hollow cylinder knob
Throw a hollow cylinder and shape the walls using the fingers of the left hand on the inside, and either the first or little finger on the outside of the wall. Squeeze them together to raise and thin the wall a little. Use a throwing rib to create a slight bevel under the base.

thick, hollow knob
This knob is hollow but has a thick wall. Use a throwing rib to form the underneath and give it the same profile as its top.

donut knob
To attach this donut-shaped knob, first use a craft knife to cut a flat area into one side. Cross-hatch the flat area of the knob as well as the lid before fixing the two together as usual. This knob does not have to be exactly central and could be placed anywhere on the lid.

Knobs thrown directly on lids

Knobs can be thrown directly onto leather-hard lids using very small balls of clay and as little water as possible. Remember that this is only a selection of what can be made using this method.

Center a leather-hard lid on the wheel (see pages 114–117). Use a craft knife to crosshatch an area in the center to create a key for the soft clay. Center (see pages 20–21) a small ball of clay onto the lid over the crosshatched area. Use the fingers to shape a knob (see below). When you are happy with the knob, carefully remove the lid from the wheel and leave to dry. If it is a solid knob, use a hole-making tool to hollow out the knob from the inside before it is completely dry.

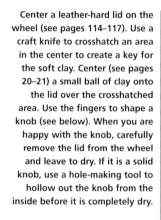

decorative knob
To make this decorative knob, form the ball of clay into a tall, solid cylinder. Use the fingers to shape concentric rings and form a point on the top.

simple knob
Use the little finger of the right hand to push under the knob to form an undercut.

hollow knob
To make this hollow knob, press a finger into the center of the revolving clay. Push down as far as the lid itself, then draw out the wall a little, supporting the wall of the knob on the outside with the left hand. Shape a small wall using the fingers to create a hollow knob.

tall, hollow knob
To make a tall, hollow knob, center a tall cylinder over the crosshatched area and use a single finger to open the clay. Throw a tall wall by squeezing together a finger of the left hand on the inside and the little finger of the right hand on the outside. Let the wall flare out at the top.

Handles as knobs

These knobs could be made from either extruded or pulled handles (see pages 148–150). The length of handle is adapted to make a series of interesting knobs. This is a sample of finished lids using handle sections. Many more complicated or unusual designs could also be created.

Hold a leather-hard, firm to the touch but still damp, lid in one hand and use a craft knife to crosshatch an area in the center to create a key. Add a little slurry to the crosshatched area to act as a glue. Lower the handle you are using as a knob (see below) onto the crosshatched area.

Smooth the handle knob onto the lid using the thumb to firmly secure it in place.

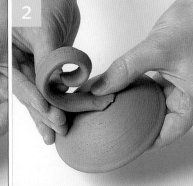

ornate knob
To make this ornate knob, coil a section of the handle around and leave it to stiffen before attaching it to the lid, otherwise it would not hold its shape.

teacup knob
Secure this handle at two points and smooth them both in the same direction.

loop knob
Push this loop knob onto the lid at two points, but do not smooth the joins. Instead, leave them as a decorative feature to create a different finish.

narrow knob
To make this narrow knob, push the loop of a handle closely together while the clay is still soft, otherwise it would crack at the top where it bends back on itself. Smooth the joins into the lid as usual.

Index

credits

The author would like to thank everyone who helped during the writing of this book, particularly Simon Blenkinship for all his support—not to mention his typing skills, her family and Simon's, who helped out in the shop, and Ian Howes, whose exeprience and excellent photography made the whole project easier.

Quarto would like to thank Potclays Limited (www.potclays.co.uk), who provided the photographs of pottery wheels on page 10.